FAMOUS HISTORICAL MYSTERIES

Also available in the Target Mystery Series:

INVESTIGATING UFOS – Larry Kettelkamp
The dramatic story of the unidentified flying object

INVESTIGATING GODS – Larry Kettelkamp
The story of the world's religions

THE STORY OF THE LOCH NESS MONSTER – Tim Dinsdale

GHOSTS, GHOULS AND OTHER HORRORS – Bernhardt J. Hurwood
50 scarifying stories of the supernatural

HAUNTED HOUSES – Bernhardt J. Hurwood

A TARGET MYSTERY

FAMOUS HISTORICAL MYSTERIES

LEONARD GRIBBLE

Illustrated by
Carl Keighley

TARGET

Target Editor: Mike Glover

Target Books is a division of Universal-Tandem Publishing Co., Ltd., 14 Gloucester Road, London SW7 4RD

'Famous Historical Mysteries' first published in Great Britain by Frederick Muller, Ltd., 1969

'More Famous Historical Mysteries' first published in Great Britain by Frederick Muller, Ltd., 1972

First published in this combined edited edition by Universal-Tandem Publishing Co., Ltd., 1974

ISBN 0 426 10428 5

Printed in Great Britain by The Anchor Press Ltd., and bound by Wm. Brendon & Son Ltd., both of Tiptree, Essex

Contents

To

H.B.
because of remembered
kindnesses and quite
a few helpful
suggestions

Introduction

The present collection of mysteries that made history in their day has been chosen to give the reader the widest range of fascinating and diverse subjects covering a period of more than five centuries, yet with several that relate to the recent past.

Not all these mysteries made the same impact upon their contemporaries, for their shapes vary as much as the concealed elements of purpose and action that made them mysterious; but all have one quality in common : they have endured to tantalize readers in the second half of the twentieth century almost as much as they challenged those to whom the first telling of these events was dramatic news of an almost incredible quality.

The passage of time has, perhaps not surprisingly, created an aura of legend around some of them, but as all were events that made strong emotional appeals to the people of their day they retain that core of unexplained mystery that endures as a challenge for later ages.

The reader of today may, in some instances, be able to offer a reasoned explanation for why these events occurred, and even how, and one that was not possible at the time when they first startled the world of their day. Therein lies much of their appeal for those of today's readers who retain a sharp curiosity about mysteries that puzzled and intrigued past generations, coupled with a strong desire to puzzle out a satisfactory and satisfying solution for themselves.

In every case the individual story's mystery is one to be evaluated by each reader for himself, which could possibly mean re-reading. It need only be said of this that just as these mysteries have been worth the retelling so they will be worth the re-reading.

That has been the verdict passed on them by history.

I

The Mystery of Kaspar Hauser

For nearly a century and a half the mystery of this youth, who was apparently unable to speak, and who suddenly appeared out of nowhere in the middle of a busy German city, has teased the minds and imaginations of historians, novelists, and playwrights.

It was on a bright Whit-Monday afternoon in May 1828, when the townsfolk of Nuremberg were abroad in the streets on holiday, that a patrolling policeman saw a crowd of youngsters gesturing and shouting at someone in their midst. The thickset Bavarian guardian of the local law strolled across to the noisy group of youths to see what had attracted their attention and given rise to their catcalls and taunting shouts. He found them gathered in a wide circle around a bewildered youth of about sixteen who was trying without much success to speak.

The youth stuttered and stammered, but no intelligible words issued from his moving lips, and there was a scared look on his face. His hair was unkempt and his clothes, which appeared home-made and very unlike the coats and trousers of the Nuremberg lads who were taunting him, were bedraggled and shapeless. When his tormentors saw the approaching policeman they ran off, releasing a fresh stream of unkind catcalls.

The frowning policeman stopped a short distance from the strange youth and ran a disapproving eye over his curious clothing.

'What's your name and where are you from?' the policeman asked.

Aware that he was being spoken to, the youth made a show of replying, but, as before, only unrecognizable sounds came from his mouth.

'Speak up and speak clearly,' the policeman ordered sharply.

Perhaps it was the sharp tone that frightened the strange youth. He suddenly threw up his arms and cowered back, as though protecting his head from expected blows. The policeman stared in disbelief as the youth stooped with a quick ducking motion of his body and picked up the hat that had been knocked from his head by his tormentors. The hat was crammed down on his unkempt hair.

It was a felt hat, round and high in the crown, and in the quick glimpse he had received of its inside the policeman had noticed that it was lined with what appeared to be red leather and yellow silk. He had seen many hats, but not one like this strange youth's.

The policeman's glance dropped to the youngster's feet. They were encased in a pair of cracked and scuffed morocco leather shoes of great age. Moreover, they had such high heels, rather like a woman's shoes, that the curious youth pitched badly when he walked, as though he was not used to the feel of them cramping his feet. There was a grubby black silk handkerchief around the skinny throat that was producing a string of unintelligible sounds, and the youth's body and legs were covered by a grey cloth jacket and worn riding-breeches.

It was quite a scarecrow to find on a May afternoon in the centre of Nuremberg.

'You'd better come along with me,' the policeman decided.

Seizing the frightened youth's arm, he turned back the way he had come and arrived at the police station with a crowd of interested sightseers trailing behind.

With the doors closed on the small crowd in the street, the spluttering and scared youth was asked a number of questions by various police officials. To every question he replied with the same unintelligible sounds.

It looked as though Nuremberg had been visited by someone who had never learned to talk!

The youth's clothes were taken from him and examined in the hope of providing a clue to his identity. The policeman, running his hand over the lining of the grey jacket, found more than just a clue. He came upon a letter that had been carefully stitched inside the grey cloth.

The letter appeared to be written in a sloping feminine hand. It was dated sixteen years previously, and was addressed to anyone who found 'the baby'. The finder was urged to take care of a child that had been discarded. The writer, presumably the child's mother, gave some guarded information when she wrote:

'I am a poor girl and cannot look after my child. His name is Kaspar Hauser. He has already been baptized. His father is dead. He was a soldier. When he is sixteen years old I beg of you to send him to Nuremberg, to the Sixth Cavalry Regiment. His father used to belong to it.'

The writer had not signed her name. However, her letter proved to be a startling document. As the chief of police pointed out when he was shown the letter, it would not have been possible for anyone writing sixteen years earlier to have known that the Sixth Cavalry Regiment would have been stationed in Nuremberg at that time.

That particular regiment had been in Nuremberg until only a few days before, when it had been ordered to leave at very short notice and quite unexpectedly.

'The letter's a forgery,' the chief of the Nuremberg police declared. 'This is borne out by the ink. It is not at all faded, as it would be after sixteen years.'

Which was a very shrewd point. But there was a complication. A second letter was found stitched into the clothes of the speechless youth. It appeared to be in a different hand, and its writer claimed to be a labourer, who stated that the boy had been given into his charge on October 7th, 1812. As the first letter claimed the boy Kaspar had been born on April 30 that year, he had been a little over five months old when the writer of the second letter became his guardian. The latter went on to explain that he had agreed to have the boy taught how to read and write, and had seen that he had been brought up a Christian, but admitted that the child had been kept in what was described as close confinement.

In short, if the letters were to be taken at face value, Kaspar Hauser was an unwanted child who had been brought up by a stranger and kept away from all normal human contacts.

Why?

The youth himself either could not or would not answer any of the fresh questions directed at him. He remained in the police station at Nuremberg, a terrible problem child for the local police to handle.

'We can't keep him unless he's charged,' the police chief pointed out to his assistants. 'So he'd better be charged as a vagrant. That will give us a chance to find out more about him.'

So the youth, with some golden down on his cheek to support the claim that he was sixteen, was taken from the police station and lodged in the Vestner Tower. As soon as his cell door clanged shut on him, the youth now known as Kaspar Hauser flung himself upon the straw bed provided by the Nuremberg authorities for the nightly comfort of vagrants and vagabonds, and without appearing in the slightest way concerned by his reception and treatment in the Bavarian city, closed his eyes, turned to face the wall, and within minutes was sleeping soundly.

He awoke to find the authorities had been in conference about the new arrival in the city. After he had been fed Kaspar was taken to be medically examined by a doctor with a stern face. More questions were shouted at him. He cringed. Questions were whispered at him, whereupon he looked confused. His body reflexes were tested. Tricks were played upon him, to take him by surprise. The process wore away most of a morning. At the end of all this the doctor pronounced his finding.

Kaspar Hauser was no more than a child in intelligence, although he was approaching puberty and his physical development fully supported the claim that he was between sixteen and seventeen years old. However, the Nuremberg doctor sensed that he had to provide some eyebrow-raising comment, so he added to his findings as a medical man his personal opinion that there must be a profound mystery at the root of this unnatural and retarded development.

After the jail mire had been cleansed from Kaspar's flesh with the other filth it had acquired, it was observed that his skin was fair and of a soft texture, unlike the skin of a working man's child. He had slender arms and legs, but they were well formed and proportioned. The boy's feet were small for his age, but their soles were as soft as the flesh of a small child. When encouraged to walk alone he was seen to stumble, somewhat in the manner of a child who has only very recently mastered how to maintain balance when putting one foot in front of the other. When a chair was put in his path he did not turn aside from it, but continued to collide with it, and then he stumbled and more often than not could not recover his lost balance, and fell down. When he fell he whimpered like a small child. It was found that he had almost no sense of how to use or employ his fingers. He held them stiffly out in front of him, and when persuaded to grasp and hold an object he used the flat of his entire hand. Although he appeared to have normal vision, his eyes appeared vacant for long periods, as though his immediate surroundings held little of interest for him. Ordinarily his facial expression was heavy, almost sullen, but when he was pleased a quick smile transformed his features, lending them a brief look of pleasant awareness.

The Nuremberg authorities transferred him to a special room, where he was observed like a specimen in a laboratory, and indeed that was really what he was, for the only way to communicate with him during the first weeks after his sudden and unexplained appearance in the city was by signs. After he had come to recognize certain signs for what they were intended to convey, an effort was made to teach him to speak. Once his interest was captured he learned with growing ease.

However, if his tongue had been left untutored for far too long, there was nothing subnormal about his memory. As his vocabulary grew so did the urge to tell what was stored in his mind. Little by little he imparted a story that was both incredible and utterly unique. He informed those who sought to unlock his store of personal history that he had lived all his life in a dark place underground, rather like a dungeon or a hermit's cell. He did not speak with the man who came to bring him food, and who was virtually his jailer. The boy explained that he had not been ill-treated, and had not been made to work or suffer hardship of any kind. He had been well fed, but the only toys he remembered playing with were made of wood, simple things constructed for a very young child. He had also been given a crudely carved wooden horse.

He had lived, for the most part, unbathed and even unwashed. He had been washed only at rare intervals which he had no way of measuring. The man who had brought him his food and drink had appeared twice during each day.

It was a stark, terribly simple story that did not take long to tell. But when his questioners again arrived at the problem of how he had come to appear in the streets of Nuremberg, they saw the former scared look return to his face, and he stood quivering and trembling in front of them.

While he had no constructive idea of where he had been kept during his solitary life underground, he had sharp impressions of the recent change in his living conditions. He had been forced to leave the place where he had been imprisoned for so long, and upon finding himself compelled to walk had discovered that he had very little sense of balance and putting one foot in front of the other had been a great effort requiring considerable concentration. When told to hurry he had fallen down.

He had been beaten for his clumsiness.

Indeed, he had only been able to totter as far as a forest before falling down exhausted. The grim-faced man accompanying him had given him a kick and hurried away. Some time later he returned driving a closed carriage. Kaspar had been helped inside and the door closed on him. It had been hot and he had been thirsty.

The carriage's wheels seemed to the youth to be rolling and bumping along for hours before the driver called to the horse and the swaying motion ceased.

The door had opened and he had been forced outside. While he stood looking in wonder at the sight of nearby houses the carriage had been driven away. Kaspar Hauser was alone in a world where he was a complete stranger.

He began stumbling towards the paved streets of Nuremberg, lost, bewildered, unable to communicate with those who approached him to stare in astonishment at this apparition that had arrived from nowhere.

That was his incredible story, drawn from him by pain-

Kaspar Hauser began stumbling towards the paved streets of Nuremberg, lost and bewildered . . .

ful process of constant inquiry. It was a story that captured the imagination not only of Germans, but of people in other European countries. Even the Nuremberg police chief, who had condemned the letter from the writer claiming to be the youth's mother as a forgery, was forced to admit that there must be more than just an element of truth in the fantastic story of a child brought up like an animal, away from human contact, so that he approached manhood with the intelligence of an infant.

It was the police chief who started the inquiry that was to end by the creation of a legend more incredible and fantastic than the halting story produced by the slow-tongued Kaspar Hauser. He had inquiries made throughout Bavaria to try to find the person or persons responsible for the child's imprisonment. The officials making the inquiries were approached by a fisherman who produced a bottle he had found two years before. Inside was a third letter. It was signed by a certain Hares Sprauka.

The writer claimed to be living a kind of Monte Cristo existence, kept in a subterranean cell in a fortress prison near Lauffenburg, on the Rhine.

The letter had no significance until one of the police inquirers started puzzling over that most unlikely signature. He found that, by rearranging the letters, he had the name Kaspar Hauser!

Yet obviously it could not have been written by the mystery youth of Nuremberg. Further inquiries were directed to Lauffenburg. Their outcome has never been made known, but it was not long after this that an attempt was made to assassinate the youth being held by the police in Nuremberg. Apparently someone was anxious that interest in his existence and past story should cease.

The would-be assassin was masked, and he broke into the room where Kaspar was sleeping and hurriedly stabbed him. The blade entered the youth's left breast. Fortunately the intruder was in a hurry, and although the stab wound resulted in a dragging illness it did not prove fatal. When the youth could be safely moved he was taken to Anspach.

By this time interest in the mysterious Kaspar Hauser was extending throughout Europe, and one Professor Daumer came forward and offered his assistance in educating the backward adolescent. An English nobleman, the Earl of Stanhope, also became interested in the fabulous story that was growing like a legend. His daughter Catherine, who later became the Duchess of Cleveland and mother of Lord Rosebery, joined her father in his desire to unravel the mystery of Kaspar Hauser. Father and daughter helped the youth in Anspach and when he was twenty secured his employment in the office of a notary named Feuerbach, and it was in this year, 1832, that research and further inquiry resulted in shaping a story about the youth's origins that still persists.

A group of researchers claimed that Kaspar Hauser was no less than the legitimate Crown Prince of Baden.

It was in the year 1812 that the infant Crown Prince vanished from the Palace of Karlsruhe on a night of wild storm, with a great wind whistling and moaning among the castle turrets. On that night one of the servants claimed he saw the White Lady in one of the many corridors. The White Lady was a ghost who was believed to appear when one of the royal family of Baden was about to die. However, the seekers after the true origin of Kaspar Hauser decided that the veiled figure seen that stormy night in Karlsruhe was no ghost, despite the servant's claim that the visitor had passed through a wall.

The person mistaken for the legendary White Lady was a woman hurrying to a secret sliding panel concealed by wall tapestries. Beyond the panel was the nursery where the infant Crown Prince slept, with two snoring nurses for night guard. The nurses, it was later claimed, had been drugged and knew nothing of the female intruder who lifted the baby from his silver cradle and substituted, in his stead, another infant that had been smuggled into the palace.

The exchanged babies were similar in age and sex. But whereas the one taken from the silver cradle was fresh-complexioned and healthy, the changeling left in his place was very pale and had ceased breathing. In short, a dead child had replaced the living infant taken from the Crown Prince's nusery.

A few hours later the Grand-Duchess Stephanie was bewailing the death of her small son. She had been told he had died suddenly and unexpectedly during that night of storm and great winds. The loss left her inconsolable, for she now believed that the heir to the throne of Baden would be not her own child, but the child of a woman she hated, the Countess von Hochberg, who had married the prince, Karl Frederick.

After the lapse of twenty years the speedy funeral of the supposed son of the Grand-Duchess Stephanie appeared to have been undertaken with what seemed to be undue haste. The mourning mother, it was said, had not been allowed to take a last glimpse of the dead child in its elaborate coffin. The reason given was that the infant had died of a contagious illness.

It was sometime after the funeral that the Grand-Duchess heard of the servant who had seen the ghost of the White Lady on the night her son had died.

She sent for the man.

'Tell me precisely what you saw that night,' she ordered.

In faltering tones the man told of seeing the cloaked female who appeared to vanish through a wall. The Grand-Duchess became convinced that she and her son had been the victims of a cruel intrigue.

If she had any doubts they were resolved when, a few days later, the servant who had told her of seeing the White

Lady was found dead in his bed. The personal physician of Karl Frederick examined the corpse.

'Death was due to apoplexy,' he announced.

After that announcement there was no further inquiry at the time into the cause of the servant's death. But the Grand-Duchess, who knew very well how much the physician was the obedient hireling of Karl Frederick, was convinced that the man she had questioned had been poisoned.

She could do nothing save grieve, for to make any overt move against the interests of the Countess von Hochberg, she knew, might mean a still greater disaster overtaking her.

But while the Grand-Duchess Stephanie remained a virtual prisoner in her own quarters of the palace, rumours began to circulate beyond its walls.

Those inquirers of a score of years later learned of the wife of a palace worker who lived a short distance from the walls. On the night the little Crown Prince was supposed to have died of a contagious disease, she told some friends and neighbours, she had sat up late suffering from toothache. It was very late that night when she heard the wheels of a carriage approaching over the cobblestones. Between howling gusts of wind she heard the carriage come to a stop, and she had looked out of a window and seen it drawn up before a small postern gate in the wall.

The woman, for a few moments, forgot the pain under her tooth as she stared with wide eyes at sight of a female figure getting down from the carriage and carrying a well-wrapped bundle in her arms. The woman alighting from the carriage was closely veiled so that her face could not be seen and she would not be recognized. The carriage remained by the postern gate until the woman reappeared, still carrying a bundle. She had entered the carriage, and as soon as the door was closed upon her the coachman drove off.

To the later inquirers it seemed that these rumours had died suddenly, almost as though killed by fear.

It was not difficult for such interested persons as Professor Daumer and the notary Feuerbach to develop a theory about what had happened that grim night of 1812 and associate events with the mysterious Kaspar Hauser.

To them it seemed that this youth was, in truth, the son and legitimate heir of the Grand-Duke Karl Frederick of Baden. The infant Crown Prince had been kidnapped from his nursery in Karlsruhe on that night twenty years before in October 1812, and the plot had been contrived and carried out by friends of the Countess von Hochberg, who wished her own son to take the place of the legitimate heir.

When the new-found friends of the young man of twenty known as Kaspar Hauser sought to unravel the mystery further, they suddenly found themselves confronted by a wall of silence. Officials who might have been expected to produce facts and records were suddenly either unwilling or unable to oblige. It was said that some of the persons making the inquiries were threatened with violence if they did not stop. However, the Earl of Stanhope, who had accepted fully the theory for which Professor Daumer was mainly responsible, was convinced that despite the failure of the authorities to find who had kept Kaspar Hauser imprisoned for more than sixteen years, and whereabouts they had done so before releasing him in Nuremberg, the Grand-Duchess Stephanie should be told the truth.

He wrote to her a very detailed letter and asked her to come to Anspach, where she could be reunited with her son.

However, the sending of that letter served as the death knell for the young man whose origin had become a topic of debate in salons throughout Europe where the liberal-minded foregathered. The Grand-Duchess received the letter and was overjoyed at the promise it held. The thought of meeting her son again after so many lost years seemed to blind her to the possibility that there could be a mistake. The letter was written with such obvious sincerity that she had no doubt that this young man, Kaspar Hauser, working as an articled clerk in a notary's office in Anspach, was the son she had so long mourned as dead.

She made arrangements to visit Anspach as soon as she could.

Unfortunately her speed was of no avail, and the woman who had once had her hopes crushed was doomed to a second brutal disappointment. She was not to see Kaspar Hauser and claim him as her son.

He died before she could reach the Bavarian town that was about thirty miles from Nuremberg, and his death was as mysterious as any feature of his curious life.

While the Grand-Duchess was actually en route to meet him, Kaspar left his lodgings in Anspach and went for a walk in a public park. It was a cold morning in December 1833, and the shrubs and blades of grass were coated with frost. Kaspar had told no one he was going to the park.

His reason for going there remained a secret until after his body had been found.

He had received earlier a letter from someone who claimed to be able to clear up, finally and without leaving any room for doubt, the riddle of his past and of his rightful identity. He was asked to keep a secret appointment in the park.

It seemed at last as if Kaspar Hauser, who had been struggling for the past five years to fit himself into a world that had burst upon him with shattering effect one day when he was sixteen, would be able to find out for himself who he was.

Whom he met on his lonely walk in the park is not known.

But later his body was found on the frozen ground. Blood

soaked his shirt-front and his coat. He had been stabbed with a slim blade like that of a stiletto. He was barely breathing when found.

While physicians tried in vain to save his life he muttered in his broken, hesitant fashion of a stranger who had come up to him and suddenly attacked him. By the time the Grand-Duchess Stephanie's coach was rumbling through the streets of the Bavarian town, Kaspar Hauser was dead.

The date was December 14th, 1833, just ten days before Christmas.

With the strange young man's death local interest died, but the legend grew. It took strength from the fact that in the dying Kaspar Hauser's pocket was found the letter which directed his steps that morning to the park where he received the fatal wound.

The Earl of Stanhope, shocked by Kaspar's violent death, offered what was then an enormous reward, a thousand pounds, for the capture and conviction of the murderer. But no one came forward with information that resulted in the killer's arrest. The Grand-Duchess Stephanie devoted years to trying to discover who had brought about the death of the young man she was convinced was her lost son. Her efforts proved useless, but they served, in their turn, to lend substance to the growing legend of Kaspar Hauser.

It was not until more than forty years later, in 1875, that a German newspaper published what was claimed to be the official record of the baptism, post-mortem, and burial of the young heir to Grand-Duke Karl Frederick, the infant son of the Grand-Duchess Stephanie. A year later the mystery was dealt with in a volume published in Heidelberg, and this proved to be source material for two German writers who were attracted by the romantic theme of a kidnapped heir and a young man appearing suddenly in a world that was quite new and strange to him.

Kurt Martens wrote a play on the subject of the Nuremberg boy which was produced in 1904, and four years later the novelist Jakob Wassermann wrote a novel around the Kaspar Hauser story. The legend was thus accepted.

But by that time, too, it had been rejected by other students of the Kaspar Hauser story. One of its severest critics was the Scottish writer Andrew Lang, who brushed aside all the so-called romantic aspect of the story. To Lang the youth who appeared in the streets of Nuremberg nearly eighty years before was a fraud. The word he used was humbug. However, he admitted the possibility that the youth suffered from some form of mental illness, which had caused him to invent, and believe in, the tale he told.

As a subject for serious-minded students the Kaspar Hauser mystery survived the First World War, and seven years after the end of the fighting a German writer produced a study of the evidence that extended to two large volumes. By that time the legend had been in existence for more than a century.

It is still alive today.

Possibly the real truth of what happened at Karlsruhe one stormy night in the early part of the nineteenth century will never be known for certain, nor will the real origin of the mysterious Kaspar Hauser be decided and determined past all doubt.

The story is unique, and its very quality of uniqueness has helped it to persist. It has attracted attention and created feelings for and against the claims made by those friends and sponsors of the young man who, if he was a fraud as Andrew Lang argued, must have been a remarkable actor.

Lang even insisted that the death in the park at Anspach was suicide. If so, it was a singularly curious time to choose, unless a young man who had successfully pulled a good deal of wool over many people's eyes had arrived at a stage where he feared eventual discovery as a fake.

However, if this was the case, it seems odd that the same young man who had persisted for four or five years to win recognition should just as suddenly throw away the final chance of acceptance by the Grand-Duchess Stephanie.

The pros and cons can be argued, as indeed they have been for a century and a half, and one is still left with doubts however much one accepts or rejects the romantic element of the story. Kaspar Hauser is today the name of a person who appeared mysteriously and whose life ended just as mysteriously. The essential mystery is rooted in the fact that nothing has been traced prior to that day in May 1828 when a group of Nuremberg youngsters began to deride and hoot at a strange-looking youth in outlandish dress who was apparently unable to speak.

It is that gap between May 1828 and October 1812, when the Crown Prince was supposed to have died, that supports the air of mystery; because no events at all in the life of Kaspar Hauser during that time have ever been proven. Had Kaspar Hauser been a complete fraud, then it should not have been impossible to trace his origins. The police chief at Nuremberg tried earnestly to find anyone who had known the youth or who was aware of his true identity. He failed.

But he failed in an age when individuals were more easily affected by so-called romantic influences and beliefs than in this far more rational age in the second half of the twentieth century.

Kaspar Hauser remains the mystery he presented to the people of Nuremberg when he first appeared among them: a youth from apparently nowhere that could be located, who died five years later on the threshold of mature manhood, leaving behind a maze of coincidences and puzzles, without entirely satisfactory explanations.

However, there is no denying the fascination of such a

unique mystery, with its dramatic moments and suggestions of either brilliant fraudulence or underhandedness in high places. For such reasons alone the mystery of who was Kaspar Hauser will doubtless continue to challenge fresh minds for a great many years to come.

2

The Mystery of the Man in the Iron Mask

On a bright summer's day in 1687 a boat put off from the shore of what is now the popular Mediterranean resort of Cannes and headed for Sainte-Marguerite, one of the two Lerin Islands, a short distance from the French coast. In front of the boat stood the provost marshal who was in charge of an armed guard surrounding a prisoner whose face could not be seen, for he kept his head lowered and wore a wide felt hat with a plume.

The boat grounded on the island's beach and the guard sprang ashore. With the provost marshal at their head, they marched towards the main entrance of the rock-girt fortress that a little over forty years before had sheltered Spanish soldiers under the command of Don Miguel Perez. It had finally been stormed by French troops led by the Comte d'Harcourt, who had taken Don Miguel prisoner and replaced the banner of St. James with the lily-decked flag of the Bourbon kings.

The guard from the boat came to a halt when their leader raised his right arm. His voice rang clearly in the warm air.

'Open in the name of King Louis!'

With a dull, grinding sound the heavy gates of the fortress swung open slowly to reveal, standing to receive the new arrivals, the newly appointed Governor of Sainte-Marguerite, Monsieur de Saint-Mars. He stared fixedly at the uniforms of the guard behind the provost marshal. They were those of the Royal Gendarmerie. Then he looked to the man they surrounded, a familiar figure who kept his head lowered so that the covering over his face could not be seen.

It was a mask concealing the face of a prisoner who had first been brought to Saint-Mars when he had been Governor of Pignerol. Each time he moved the prisoner followed him under heavy guard, like a phantom.

The provost marshal made his formal announcement. 'I am delivering into your custody, monsieur, a masked prisoner who will remain masked so long as he is in your charge. This is an order from the King.'

The prisoner lifted his head, and Saint-Mars saw the familiar sight of the man who has become known to history as the Man in the Iron Mask. Through the eye slits he could feel the hard gaze. He cleared his throat and spoke to his own waiting guard inside the gates. They moved forward to take the prisoner from the provost marshal's guard.

Some minutes later the great fortress gates clanged shut again, closing on the new prisoner and his regular custodian.

They also closed like a vice on the mystery of the man with the masked face who had been handed into the safe keeping of the governor of that lonely prison in the Mediterranean.

Sainte-Marguerite was one of a pair of small islands off the French coast known as the Iles des Lérins. They were specks in the sea with a romantic past, for hundreds of years before the coming of the Man in the Iron Mask aristocrats of the Roman Empire had built seaside villas on them. In those days the islands had been known as Lero and Lerina, and above the Roman villas rose temples of marble.

By the fourth century A.D. the villas and temples were crumbling and snakes invaded the ruins. For more than

Saint-Mars saw the familiar sight of the man who has become known to history as the Man in the Iron Mask.

a hundred years the islands were twin wildernesses, forgotten and neglected. They had not only gone out of fashion. They had gone from living memory.

Then a man named Honorat, born in Gaul of noble Roman parents, came to one of the islands. He had been converted to Christianity and felt an overwhelming impulse to live the pious life of a hermit, away from his fellows. He chose the little snake-infested island in the Mediterranean sunshine as a place where he could devote himself to prayer and contemplation. But the snakes interrupted his devotions.

Honorat prayed for divine assistance in overcoming the snakes, and as a result performed his first miracle on Lerina. He addressed himself to the snakes and within a short while all were dead. The miracle was completed when a tidal wave, completely unknown hitherto in the landlocked Mediterranean, swept over the islands. When the swirling waters fell back they bore away the dead snakes. However, with the snakes gone, Honorat found his small island had no drinking water. Again he prayed for help, and this time he was directed to a secret place where a well had been dug. Its water was fresh and clear and cool.

To the other island journeyed Honorat's sister, Marguerite, who had decided that she must live a similar life of devotion. After landing on Lero she felt she must tell her brother what she had done. So she crossed to Lerina, and brother and sister agreed never to visit each other or interrupt their devotions by crossing from one island to the other except when the cherry trees were in bloom.

Honorat and Marguerite were made saints, and according to an ancient legend the cherry trees of the Lerin Islands bloomed every month during their lifetime. Lerina's name was changed to Saint-Honorat and Lero became renamed Sainte-Marguerite, the names by which they are still known.

The Man in the Iron Mask probably saw no cherry trees in bloom during the eleven years he remained in the fortress prison of Sainte-Marguerite. His life became a dull routine, broken only by the occasional visit from Monsieur de Saint-Mars, the governor; he was just as much a prisoner as the mystery man who was in his charge and whose curious mask was never loosened and removed. None of the jailers saw the mystery man's face. The words he spoke to them came muffled so that they could not know the real sound of his voice. When they heard him moaning in moments of despair they crossed themselves and hastened out of earshot.

The years passed with little disturbance. Sainte-Marguerite and its mystery prisoner of State alike seemed forgotten again by the Sun King and his Court. But one day something occurred which filled Monsieur de Saint-Mars with fear. That was the day a fisherman, drawing in his net from the sea under the wall of the fortress, found among the fish and weeds he had dredged up something that gleamed brightly.

It was a silver plate with little marks scratched across its bright surface, as though with a knife point, little marks that the fisherman realized was writing. Someone had scratched a message across the plate and flung it into the sea in the one place where it might be found.

However, the fisherman could not read.

He took the plate with its message to Monsieur de Saint-Mars and explained how he had come to find it. The Governor of Sainte-Marguerite looked at the scratch marks on the plate for a long time before asking his first question.

'Have you read the message on this plate?'

The fisherman shook his head. 'I cannot read, your honour,' he confessed.

Saint-Mars looked at him sternly.

'Have you shown this plate to anyone else?' he asked.

'I brought it directly to you, your honour,' the fisherman replied, 'as soon as I had landed my catch.'

'Why to me?'

'I saw that on it.'

The fisherman pointed to a fleur-de-lis crest on the plate That crest was the royal sign of the Bourbons.

It is said Saint-Mars gave the fisherman a piece of gold and told him, 'Take this and forget what you have found. Just remember that you are a terribly lucky man.'

Looking from the golden louis in his hand to the still stern governor of the prison, the fisherman asked, 'You mean I am a lucky man to be paid in gold, your honour?'

'No,' said Saint-Mars. 'You are lucky because you cannot read.'

Was the message of the silver plate a desperate plea thrown into the space outside his dungeon wall slit by the Man in the Iron Mask? Even the plate with the royal crest and its unknown message have passed into legend that only makes the curious mystery more baffling.

Saint-Mars was a man who could keep a secret, especially a royal one. His long vigil over his unknown prisoner was in due course rewarded when he was promoted from Governor of the lonely island of Sainte-Marguerite to Governor of the most dread and frightening fortress prison in France, the notorious Bastille, in Paris.

However, there was a condition attaching to this promotion. When Saint-Mars left the sunshine of the Mediterranean for the gloom of the Bastille he did not travel alone. He was accompanied by his very special prisoner, the Man in the Iron Mask.

On this point there was no room for doubt, for seventy-one years later, exactly twenty years before a mob stormed the Bastille and so made the first violent move in what was to grow into the French Revolution, a diary was published in Paris. It was a slim volume of personal memories by a certain Etienne de Jonca, who had been appointed a lieutenant at the Bastille at the time of the arrival of Iron Mask. He had died three years after the mysterious prisoner.

In the diary appeared the following entry for September 18th, 1698:

'At three o'clock in the afternoon Monsieur de Saint-Mars, Governor of the Bastille, arrived from the island of Sainte-Marguerite. He brought with him in a litter one of his former prisoners at Pignerol whose name is not mentioned and who is constantly masked. On his arrival he was put in the Tour de la Basinière till dark. At nine in the evening I conducted him myself to the third room in the Tour de la Bertaudière, which I had taken care to furnish properly before his arrival, according to an order received by me from Monsieur de Saint-Mars. In conducting him, I was accompanied by Monsieur de Rosarges, who came with Monsieur de Saint-Mars, and took care of and attended the prisoner whose table was furnished by the governor.'

Unfortunately Etienne de Jonca did not feel, at that time, that it was necessary to enlarge upon the subject of the mysterious prisoner. He remained a lieutenant of the Bastille for the next five years, at the end of which time he made another entry in his personal journal. In this entry he referred to the prisoner's mask, but did not give him a name.

The entry read:

'Monday, November 19th, 1703. The unknown prisoner, whom Monsieur de Saint-Mars brought with him from the island of Sainte-Marguerite, where he had been a long time under his care, and who has always been masked with a mask of black velvet, found himself worse yesterday, in coming from Mass, and died this evening at ten o'clock without any great illness. Monsieur Girault, our chaplain, confessed him yesterday; his death being sudden, he had not an opportunity of taking the Sacraments, but our chaplain exhorted him a few minutes before he expired. He was buried on Tuesday, November 20th, in the burying place of our parish of St. Paul. His burial cost forty livres.'

A brief statement about the passing of an unknown whose identity remains one of the great mysteries of history. But in making it de Jonca added his own piece of mystery. He had referred to a velvet mask that was always worn by the prisoner, not a mask of metal. Historians and more romantically minded writers have argued about the material of which this mask was made for more than two hundred and fifty years. Some have accepted de Jonca's description; others, like Alexandre Dumas, supported the claim that the mask was indeed of iron. It is more than likely that the mask was a cruel device with a metal collar and metal stays to which a concealing pad of shaped velvet was fastened, to make it possible for the person wearing it to eat and breathe. But a material such as velvet would have worn out with day-to-day use, and there is no record of the mask being renewed or having to be. Apart from de Jonca's private note made at the time of the unknown's death there is no factual proof, only legend that is as enduring as iron itself.

However, the parish register of St. Paul contains an entry that actually gives the mystery prisoner a name. Unfortunately the name in this entry merely serves to confuse rather than clarify the prisoner's identity.

This register entry reads:

'In the year 1703, on the 19th day of November, Marchiali, aged forty-five years or thereabouts, died at the Bastille. His body was interred in the burying place of this parish of St. Paul on the 20th of the said month, in the presence of Monsieur de Rosarges, Major of the Bastille, and Monsieur Reilh, the surgeon, who accordingly sign this.'

Neither of the Bastille officials who signed the register had the name Marchiali altered, but so far as can be traced no one of that name could have been the prisoner known to history as the Man in the Iron Mask.

On the other hand, it is known that Saint-Mars did have in his keeping for long periods two prisoners whose names were Douger and Mattioli. Saint-Mars was the governor of three fortress prisons before being appointed Governor of the Bastille. He spent the years from 1664 to 1681 in charge of the jail at Pignerol, then for six years he was the Governor of Exiles, moving on in 1687 to Sainte-Marguerite. He remained Governor of the Bastille until his death, when a great many secrets passed away with him.

One of these was the real identity of the Man in the Iron Mask.

What is known is that Saint-Mars invariably treated the masked mystery prisoner with the greatest respect, as though he were of royal blood or were a State prisoner of high rank.

Why the prisoner at Pignerol named Douger, who was arrested in 1669, was thrown into jail and apparently forgotten is not known. But he was without doubt in Saint-Mars' custody at Pignerol. So was Mattioli, arrested ten years later, in 1679. The likelihood is that one of these men was the notorious Iron Mask, who followed Saint-Mars each time he changed governorship. Allowing for a possible misspelling of the name Mattioli in the St. Paul's parish register, it would seem that de Jonca had heard of Mattioli arriving at Pignerol while Saint-Mars was governor and had heard, furthermore, that no reference was to be made to the prisoner's identity. So no such reference was made in his journal, even after five years. But a name had to be given to the clerk who filled in the parish register and procured the signatures of the surgeon and the officer described as the major. De Jonca could have been the officer who supplied the few details necessary for the entry in the parish register.

However, even this is not conclusive. It would seem to put too much emphasis on a mere clerical error.

Saint-Mars himself aided, rather than otherwise, the growing confusion about his masked prisoner's identity. Indeed, he frequently wrote about him, but always referred to him as the Mask or the Man in the Mask, and on one occasion he confessed that he had deliberately circulated stories about the prisoner that were untrue. His description of these was 'fairy tales', in the circumstances not the most suitable of terms.

But Saint-Mars could have had a reason for behaving in this deliberately misleading manner. It is possible that he did not know his prisoner's identity, but was trying to show whoever was responsible for the man being put in his charge that he was actively working to prevent anyone from discovering who the Mask really was.

That the prisoner was a high-ranking prisoner of State, whose identity had to be kept a secret for State purposes, was of course known to the man who became his chief guardian from the time he arrived at Pignerol, in Piedmont. For the prisoner to escape, or for his identity to become known, would have meant death for Saint-Mars. So far as it is known, he treated his prisoner politely and did his best to make the unknown's lengthy imprisonment bearable. After all, the prisoner might be released one day. That could be a sad day for Saint-Mars if the released man, free of his mask, remembered only suffering and hardship.

Undoubtedly the legend about the masked prisoner began with Saint-Mars himself, who did not describe the actual mask. It was the famous French writer Voltaire, who was responsible for continuing the legend that the prisoner was, in fact, a natural brother of Louis XIV, who was imprisoned by the King so that he could not become a rival for the throne of France. Voltaire also claimed the prisoner's peculiar mask, which was a kind of total headgear, was actually made of iron.

From that day the mystery prisoner was, to the French, *Masque de Fer*—Iron Mask. To the rest of the world he became the Man in the Iron Mask.

Dumas, a well known novelist, took over the Voltaire claim and wrote a novel around the idea of a twin brother of Louis XIV who was imprisoned when he grew up and kept with his face always concealed by a mask made of iron.

Such a mystery prisoner was explained away by other writers who were challenged by the peculiar circumstances. The mother of Louis XIV, Anne of Austria, was said to have had a son by the English Duke of Buckingham at the time of his visit to France in 1625. The baby was, according to this claim, taken from the royal apartments by the French statesman, Cardinal Mazarin, who made himself responsible for the child's upbringing and education. Mazarin died in 1661, and afterwards the King had the Cardinal's charge, who was thirteen years older than Louis, imprisoned after a mask-like piece of special headgear had been riveted to the prisoner's neck.

For the believers in this theory there is the period of years between 1661 and 1679 to be explained, if that was the year when the Man in the Iron Mask first was handed over to the care of Saint-Mars. In any case, as other writers have pointed out, this theory would have had the prisoner over eighty years of age at the time of his death in the Bastille. This is extremely unlikely and runs counter to the evidence of de Jonca.

Others have claimed that, while this story is true in the main, and that Cardinal Mazarin did in fact take care of a child born to Anne of Austria, it was Mazarin himself who was the boy's father. This claim is even less likely except in one particular. The claimants argue that this child was born in 1644, a much more likely date than twenty years earlier.

More fanciful theorists suggest that the Man in the Iron Mask himself became a father, and that his son was smuggled away to the island of Corsica where he became known as de Buona Parte, married in due course, and so founded a family that later produced another child who was destined to become famous—Napoleon Bonaparte.

But such a theory is little more than a flight of fancy, and certainly the republican artillery officer who later became Emperor of the French had no illusions about being descended from royal blood.

He looked upon the House of Bourbon as his arch-enemy.

The masked prisoner has also been identified as at least two other French noblemen. One was the Duc de Beaufort, the second son of another duke, the Duc de Vendôme, who was descended from the royal house as an illegitimate son of that warlike Henry of Navarre who decided Paris was worth a Mass and became Henry IV.

But this claim falls down on close examination, for the Duc de Beaufort was born in 1611, and was killed nearly sixty years later by the Turks, in June 1669, at the siege of Candia. This was said to have been witnessed by the Marquis de Saint-André Montbrun. However, the slaughtered duke's body was never recovered, and it is probably for this reason that the rumours began which linked him to the unknown masked prisoner. But an examination of the relative dates shows that this possibility is even less likely than the claim that the masked prisoner was the son of the Duke of Buckingham.

Another royal personality fitted to the legend, although imperfectly, is the Comte de Vermandois, who was the son of Louis XIV and the Duchesse de la Vallière. But he was born as late as 1667.

He died in 1683, when only sixteen, according to the records, but although Louis loved this son it is known that on more than one occasion he made his father terribly angry by actions which were never explained to the Court.

Even more unlikely is the claim that the Man in the Iron Mask was none other than the great dramatist, Jean Molière, whose plays attacked the society of his day. He is said to have gravely upset the King, who decided to teach him a lesson he could take the rest of his life to learn.

But there is no foundation for this idea, and in any case Molière was born in 1622 and was over fifty when he died in 1673. Such a prisoner would not have lived at Pignerol or on Sainte-Marguerite without writing and what he wrote would not have been lost to the world unless it was deliberately destroyed. There is no record of Saint-Mars having works by his prisoner burned.

Not everyone believed that the Man in the Iron Mask was a Frenchman. At one time there was a strong claim put forward that the masked prisoner whose identity was never revealed by Saint-Mars was the English Duke of Monmouth, whose Protestant army was defeated at the battle of Sedgemoor, in Somerset, in 1685. Monmouth was a natural son of Charles II and he was sentenced to be executed for leading the rebellion against his uncle, James II. A legend grew up about a substitution of another prisoner for Monmouth on the day he was to be executed in London on Tower Hill. According to rumours circulating soon after Monmouth bowed under the headsman's axe before a great crowd, his uncle the King had made a secret pact with the King of France to conceal his ill-advised nephew. Once Monmouth was in France, King Louis decided his face must never be seen by any who could recognize him. So he became the Man in the Iron Mask.

The entire legend was given considerable support by two persons, a Frenchman and an Englishwoman. The former, Saint-Foix, said that, shortly before his death, Charles II had made his brother James swear that, whatever Monmouth did he should never be called to answer for his actions with his life. According to Saint-Foix, James had agreed to this.

The Englishwoman's part in furthering this legend of Monmouth being the Man in the Iron Mask was much more direct. She claimed to have had Monmouth's grave opened secretly, and to have been shocked by seeing a stranger's face on the severed head. She was Lady Wentworth, whose word carried considerable weight, but if she did peek into Monmouth's coffin she very likely saw the result of shock and muscular distortion on familiar features wasted by death, which made them appear a stranger's and for her, in her undoubted highly emotional state, unrecognizable, as those of the unfortunate James, Duke of Monmouth. If Monmouth had only waited three years he might have paraded his army to London without having to strike a blow. But if he was, in truth, the Man in the Iron Mask he must have suffered agonies when, in 1688, the Protestants William of Orange and his Stuart wife Mary landed at Lyme Regis to be named King and Queen while James II took the first ship available to sail for France and exile.

The widespread belief that Iron Mask was a man with some kind of English background continued when other claimants advanced the theory that the famous prisoner was Eustache Douger, who was sent to Pignerol, where he is known to have acted for a time as valet to another prisoner. This was Nicholas Fouquet, who had received a life sentence for robbing the State of a vast fortune while in charge of national finances under Cardinal Mazarin.

Douger—or Dauger, as the name is sometimes spelled—was no more than a false name, according to those who believe he was Iron Mask. They have given him the identity of an Abbé Pregnani, who was known to have been in England at one time trying to convert Charles II to Roman Catholicism. He was unsuccessful, and returned to the Continent via Dunkirk, where he was supposedly seized and sent secretly to Pignerol. Some of the supporters of this theory have even advanced the suggestion that the Abbé Pregnani was able to obtain such close audience with the English king because he was actually Charles's son.

Much more likely is the now generally held belief that the mysterious prisoner was an Italian count named Mattioli, who became one of the Duke of Mantua's principle ministers and was the chief architect of a plan to lease a frontier fortress to the French at a price. The fortress was the important one of Casale, and the price was a hundred thousand crowns.

The French king was not against making the deal. However, he not only lost interest in it, but became angry with Mattioli when he learned that, on behalf of the Duke of Mantua, the count was setting up a league of Italian States to challenge the leadership of France.

Secret agents were sent by Louis to kidnap the double-dealing Italian. He was to be brought back to France alive.

The men despatched from France crossed into Italy and eventually came up with Count Mattioli in Turin, where he was making an attempt to persuade the Duke of Savoy to join the proposed Italian league.

He was seized and spirited out of the city and back across the French frontier. To ensure that the truth of this secret mission never became known, Louis ordered the new prisoner of State to be masked and imprisoned at Pignerol. However, the secret of the kidnapping was breached when, a few years later, an account of the Casale conspiracy was related in a volume published in Cologne. In this the story of the kidnapping of the man who broke faith with Louis was told for the first time.

If the Duke of Mantua made any protest to King Louis about the treatment of Mattioli no record exists today, for twenty-eight years after the incident Mantua was captured by the Austrian troops of Prince Eugene, who was an ally of Marlborough's in the War of the Spanish Succession, and in that same year, 1707, he had most of the Mantua State records sent to Vienna. Later they vanished.

From that time a conspiracy of silence seemed to involve anyone who might know the truth. Saint-Mars, according to an elderly official at the time of the French Revolution, had hinted to his father that the masked prisoner had been at one time a minister at the Court of Turin. But there was no further support for the claim that Saint-Mars had broken the habit of a lifetime.

Louis XV was equally silent on the subject except, according to rumour, when he spoke of the famous prisoner to the Duc de Choiseul, a favourite of his. Even then, the rumour claimed, he merely hinted that the unknown was a minister from an Italian state. But this may have been no more than fitting a piece of an incomplete jigsaw puzzle into a missing space.

All the same, the weight of evidence points to the Man in the Iron Mask being the kidnapped count, and to the mask being of velvet, at least in the later years of his life. Support for this was provided by a fellow-officer who served at the Bastille with de Jonca. His name was Chevalier, and after the masked prisoner had been buried he related how his room in the fortress prison was virtually destroyed to remove all trace of his lonely stay. Its walls were thoroughly scraped, the ceiling pulled down, and the floor-boards removed and burned with the furniture. All metal fixings and tableware were removed and melted down. In this way any trace of his having existed was destroyed. His clothes and mask were burned.

Yet it is a fact, as another prisoner from Sainte-Marguerite confirmed, that the masked man ate his meals from a silver plate, was treated with some respect by Saint-Mars, the governor, who also provided the unknown with costly clothes. Moreover, the man in the mask spoke several languages in a cultured voice and was grey-haired.

Beyond a few details such as these one can only guess. There was a chance of learning the truth at the time of the taking of the Bastille, on July 14th, 1789, but secret records were destroyed or vanished and nothing remained in the masked prisoner's room in the Tour de la Bertaudière to point to his ever having spent five years and two months there, concealed from the world that had known him.

3

The Mystery of the *Mary Celeste*

In the year 1861, that saw the opening of the American Civil War, a small sailing vessel called a brigantine was built on the stocks of a shipbuilding yard in Parrsborough, on the coast of Nova Scotia. Just before she was ready for launching a sign-writer was told to climb over her bows and paint her name. It was a rather warlike name: *Amazon*.

Not that the new ship looked very warlike, even in a feminine way. She had two masts and her length was just two feet under an even hundred. Her beam was a quarter of her length, twenty-five feet. She was of modest tonnage. It was registered as 282 tons.

When at last she glided down the slipway and rode for the first time with her keel under water she did not look like a vessel whose future would be clouded in mystery. But today she is remembered as a vessel whose name became associated with one of the most puzzling mysteries of the sea.

But that name is not *Amazon*.

It is an age-long superstition among deep-sea sailormen that to change a ship's name is to invite bad luck to attend the rest of her career.

After the *Amazon* had been in service for some years as a sailing vessel carrying general cargo up and down the Atlantic seaboard and occasionally to Europe she was sold and her new owners had her name changed. The old name was painted out, and instructions were given for the name *Mary Sellers* to be substituted.

Possibly the new sign-writer was a French-Canadian. In any case, he must have misunderstood his instructions, for the name he painted on the brigantine was *Mary Celeste*. A curious name, half English, half French. Indeed, for many years after the mystery attending one of her voyages across the Atlantic, she was known as the *Marie Celeste*, an all-French name. But this name was incorrect, although she is often referred to in modern times by that mistaken name.

For eleven years she ploughed the Atlantic sea lanes familiar to her until she brought up, in November 1872, in New York, and when the gangplank was lowered her master, Captain Benjamin S. Briggs, went ashore to see the agents and learn what cargo she was to take aboard and where she was to sail it.

Captain Briggs was not only the brigantine's master; he was part owner. His home was aboard the *Mary Celeste*. When her anchor was brought up and her sails were unfurled Mrs. Briggs and her young daughter who was two years old when the *Mary Celeste* tied up in New York on that November day, moved into the captain's quarters.

The agent greeted Captain Briggs with a friendly nod and told him of the cargo waiting to be moved to the *Mary Celeste*'s hold.

'It's commercial alcohol this time, Captain. You're to deliver it in Genoa.'

Whatever he felt at this news, Captain Briggs could not have been overjoyed. There were less tricky cargoes to be carried than alcohol, whatever its quality, and there were more pleasing routes to be followed than crossing the Atlantic with winter coming on in a slow sailing vessel whose deck could be covered from stem to stern in thirty good paces.

'How soon do you want me to sail?' he asked the agent.

'As soon as her hatches are battened down. We'll start loading without delay.'

That evening the *Mary Celeste*'s master told his wife, 'I'm going to see Moorhouse. I saw the *Dei Gratia* was in port. David will expect me to look in on him.'

He went ashore, found his friend Captain David Moorhouse of the brigantine *Dei Gratia*, and the two sailing masters had dinner together. Neither knew it was the last time they would see and talk to each other. Yet, by one of those coincidences that often happen in real life, and make it even more absorbing than the most carefully plotted fiction, it was to be Captain Moorhouse who first gave to the world the story of the mystery surrounding his friend's ship and her crew.

The next day seventeen hundred barrels of commercial alcohol were taken aboard the *Mary Celeste* and stowed in her hold. The weather turned bad. Captain Briggs, who had spent his life at sea, was thirty-seven years old, and had used his savings to buy a share in his command, decided it would be too risky to head for the open ocean. He dropped anchor off Staten Island, in the mouth of New York harbour, and waited until the weather changed.

He had to wait two days. That was anything but a promising beginning for the voyage.

However, on November 7th the weather changed. The wind dropped and the sea grew calmer. Captain Briggs gave the order for the brigantine's anchor to be raised and stowed. A short while later the *Mary Celeste* was dipping her bows and heading in an easterly direction on a southerly tack, bound for the Mediterranean and the Italian port of Genoa, the birthplace of Columbus.

As the *Mary Celeste*'s topsails vanished over the horizon she was sailing into a mystery that still challenges many to solve it.

One of the first to accept the challenge was David Moorhouse. When he left New York he was carrying a cargo to be landed at Gibraltar. Like Captain Briggs, he had to take note of the prevailing weather conditions, and he too started on a southerly tack.

Crossing the Atlantic in those days by sail could take up to a month. Already the early steamships were cutting down the time, but the sailing-ships carrying general cargo were cheap and, despite the longer time taken on voyage, they could still compete with the new steamers as carriers of merchandise.

It was almost a month after the *Mary Celeste* had up-anchored off Staten island that the lookout on Captain Moorhouse's *Dei Gratia* reported a sail. The time was around three in the afternoon of December 5th, 1872. Before very long the light would be failing. There was a smudge of smoke against the sky far to starboard, where a German steamer continued her course to the West Indies.

Her captain had signalled to the sailing vessel just reported by the *Dei Gratia*'s lookout, but had received no answering signal. He had decided to continue on course.

Captain Moorhouse signalled, and he too received no reply. He gave orders to his second mate, named Wright, to move closer to the other sailing vessel, while he studied her through his telescope.

As the *Dei Gratia* altered course her captain noted the deserted deck of the vessel he was overhauling. There was no one at her wheel, and she was yawing badly. There was no distress signal flying from her masthead, but Captain Moorhouse had a feeling that something was very wrong with the ship seen through his telescope. Her flapping canvas and deserted appearance hundreds of miles from the nearest land, in a position south-east of the Azores, looked like trouble.

He kept the telescope trained on her until he could make out her name.

There was no one at her wheel, and she was yawing badly.

Mary Celeste.

Captain Moorhouse closed his telescope with a snap.

'Mr. Deveau!' he called.

The first mate came hurrying.

'You will take a boat and boarding party,' Captain Moorhouse told him, 'and find out why that brigantine appears deserted.'

'Aye-aye, sir,' said the *Dei Gratia*'s first mate, and turned away, calling to some of the crew.

The light was growing poorer as the *Dei Gratia*'s boat covered the distance between the two brigantines alone in mid-Atlantic. Captain Moorhouse watched his men climbing aboard the other ship, and waited impatiently for Deveau to return and report what he had found.

It was a puzzled and unhappy first mate who returned to seek out his captain and tell him of the mystery of a ship deserted by her crew with no apparent reason for their leaving. Deveau had found no one aboard the *Mary Celeste.* Her single boat, big enough to carry her crew of seven as well as the captain and his wife and baby daughter, was no longer held on its davits.

In the short time he had been aboard Deveau had run a critical seaman's eye over the state of the deserted ship. He had found almost nothing wrong with her. There was some damage to the bows, but it hadn't looked serious. There was also a good three feet of seawater swilling about the barrels in the hold, but that was not a danger level, and so far as Deveau had been able to tell she was not dangerously shipping water.

Moreover, there were plenty of supplies aboard. The quick glance he had taken had shown supplies for about six months. He had looked into the captain's quarters. There he had seen a pipe on a ledge and some pieces of feminine jewellery on a shelf, items one would have expected the captain and his wife to pick up if they were in a hurry to make a sudden departure from the brigantine.

Deveau had even noticed some of the Briggs baby's toys lying on a cabin floor, where presumably they had been left when the child ceased playing with them. He had opened a cupboard door to be confronted by clothing belonging to the captain and Mrs. Briggs hanging normally from their pegs.

Indeed, everything aboard the *Mary Celeste* seemed normal. This was the basic mystery surrounding the ship and what had occurred to send her occupants away in the only boat – if that was how they had left her.

When Captain Moorhouse heard of what his first mate had found aboard his friend's ship he decided to take the *Mary Celeste* into port.

'We'll put a party aboard her, Mr. Deveau,' he declared, 'and we'll take her to Gib. You'll go back and steer her.'

'We'll lose time,' the first mate pointed out.

'That can't be helped. She's deserted, we'll salvage her, and they can start arguing about her when we tie up and the Gib harbour master comes aboard.'

Captain Moorhouse paused, giving his first mate a hard glance, and asked, 'What do you think happened, Mister?'

Deveau shook his head.

'I can't be sure of course,' he said. 'But I noticed that their sounding rod was lying near the pumps, Captain.'

'You think they were worried about the water in the hold? That it?'

'I think they were led to believe the water was rising, and as there was a woman and her child aboard the captain gave the order to take to the boat.'

'You'll have to appear before a salvage court, Mister,' Captain Moorhouse reminded the first mate. 'Is this what you'll tell them,'

Deveau nodded. 'Aye, sir. This is what I believe must have happened.'

'How long ago?'

'That I can't say till I've made another examination,' said the first mate.

He had plenty of time to make up his mind on the long haul to Gibraltar. But it was a puzzling task, as he discovered when he examined the neatly kept log book, found in its regular place, but only made up to some ten days before she was taken in tow by the *Dei Gratia*. The entries were typical seamen's notes, containing little information, and there were not more than seven of them made from the time the *Mary Celeste* had pulled eastwards from Staten Island.

One entry said briefly, 'Got in Royals and top G. sail,' leaving any mariner reading it to understand why. Another, apparently referring to the *Mary Celeste*'s course, if not to the prevailing wind, was 'E.S.E.' (east-south-east).

The one word 'Rainy' was a third entry. '9 knots' was one referring to the vessel's speed.

The last position recorded was '36 N 56, 27 W 20'. The day was November 24th, the last day the log book was brought up to date, in any sense of the term. There was, however, a chalked record on the nearby slate. This was for the next day. The chalk entries on the slate were normally copied at a convenient time later into the log book. That had been the usual custom in such sailing-ships for a great many years.

The chalk entry on the *Mary Celeste*'s slate gave the additional information to the puzzled Deveau that at eight o'clock in the morning of the following day after the last log book entry had been made the brigantine was six miles north-north-east beyond the eastern tip of one of the Azores islands. This was the small island of Santa Maria.

It naturally occurred to him to consider the possibility that the captain and crew of the *Mary Celeste* had abandoned ship shortly after that chalked information was made on the slate. But ten days earlier the level of the water in the hold would probably have been lower than it was when the sounding rod was dropped beside the pumps. There was no valid reason that the first mate of the *Dei Gratia* could see for assuming that the *Mary Celeste* had been deserted as long as ten days before she was found.

There was also the detail of her sails at the time Captain Moorhouse stood viewing her coming closer in his telescope. She was on a port tack at the time, yawing wildly, but her foretopmast-staysail and jib were set to starboard. She would hardly have reached the position where she was found under such a rig, for Captain Moorhouse had logged his own ship's position at the time of coming up with the *Mary Celeste*.

This was 38 N 20, 17 W 15. In short, she was five hundred miles from Santa Maria in the Azores. Only the capable handling of her crew could have brought her across that distance. However, to writers not so sea-minded as Deveau and his captain, there has apparently been a curious land-lubber's logic in claiming that the missing boat was lowered, and the ship's company left in it, shortly after that last chalk mark was made on the logging slate.

On the journey to Gibraltar a further survey was taken of the state of the *Mary Celeste*, and some new items of interest were discovered.

Apparently Benjamin Briggs had left in the ship's boat with his crew and family, taking with him some of the *Mary Celeste*'s stores, but not enough for a long journey. However, he had been careful to collect, before stepping into the launched boat, his sextant, which would be a necessary aid to navigating, especially in winter, and also the *Mary Celeste*'s ship's papers, a matter that would be of deep concern to the master of any ship.

But he had not pocketed his watch before leaving, and he had not bothered to pick up some loose money found in his cabin. In the crew's quarters there was the same apparent readiness to forego personal items when leaving the *Mary Celeste*, and perhaps it was more marked in their case, for sailormen received little in cash pay a hundred years ago.

The *Mary Celeste*'s crew had left their sea-chests, a costly item among any sailor's personal effects, and there was no sign of the chests being rifled or hurriedly emptied. In each case the chest remained with its contents neatly arranged. Sailormen usually took the trouble to pocket their favourite pipe. But several pipes were found in the crew's quarters, as well as rolls of tobacco.

There had, in fact, been no attempt to remove the kind of personal possessions one would have expected the members of the crew to push into their pockets before leaving the ship.

But one interesting factor was the hatch cover that had been removed and was found lying on its other side. Added to the additional factor of a barrel below that open hatch being found damaged, it was to invite a number of widely varying theories about what had happened, ranging from alcohol fumes blowing off the hatch cover and creating panic, to the crew having forced open the hold and reached the alcohol, their first stage towards outright mutiny.

This last picture of events was at first supported by the cutlass that was found lying on the deck. The weapon's blade had some dark red stains on the weathered steel. Unfortunately for the theorists with lively imaginations these stains were later, in Gibraltar, found to be no more alarming than rust.

However, once such a theory had been expressed, it took hold. Mutiny at sea followed by complete mystery as to what became of mutineers and victims was too exciting a story to be given up easily. Although it has generally been considered as convincingly disproved by other factors and considerations, it nevertheless continued for a great many years, and there are still books available where the mutiny theory is upheld by the writer and claimed to be supported by the few known facts.

Possibly an offshoot of the mutiny theory was the claim that the men shipped as crew aboard the *Mary Celeste* were cut-throats from the American eastern seaboard. The story of one of the barrels of raw alcohol being found damaged was good enough to start, at a later date, the rumour that the villainous crew had tampered with the cargo and after becoming drunk on the crude spirit ran amok, murdering the captain and his family. But the theory does not explain what happened to the occupants who launched the *Mary Celeste*'s boat and apparently rowed away from her pitching side.

Even launching that boat was not accomplished without, seemingly, some difficulty, for part of the deckrail had had to be cut away. The severed section of rail was left lying on the deck. But all that can be said of this detail is that it displays determination to be away from the *Mary Celeste* and does not point to why she was deserted nor where the occupants of the boat hoped to make for.

The fact that Captain Briggs had taken with him, besides his sextant and ship's papers, his ship's chronometer and navigation book suggests that he had hopes of successfully voyaging in the small boat towards the known sea lanes, his one hope of being picked up in the Atlantic in December.

The *Dei Gratia* sailed into the harbour at Gibraltar in the evening of December 12th. The *Mary Celeste*, with Deveau at the helm, arrived some hours later, on the morning of 13th, to be welcomed by a curious crowd of spectators who watched her drop anchor as though she were a ghost ship. Already the story of her being found deserted was common knowledge on the Rock, and the authorities were making the first moves to set up a court of inquiry.

The salvage court ultimately awarded Captain Moorhouse and the *Dei Gratia*'s crew the sum of seventeen hundred pounds for salvaging the deserted *Mary Celeste* and bringing her to port. A curious figure. It amounted to a pound for each barrel of commericial alcohol in the *Mary Celeste*'s holds.

From the western side of the Atlantic came James Winchester to take possession of the salvaged brigantine. He was the chief owner, and he was able to tell those directly interested in solving the mystery of the deserted ship that Benjamin Briggs, whom he had known for a good many years, was a ship's master who allowed no drinking of alcohol aboard his vessel.

He had an interview with David Moorhouse, whose reputation as a ship's master was known to him. He spoke to Deveau and various members of the *Dei Gratia*'s crew who had been aboard the *Mary Celeste*. He inspected the vessel himself.

As a result of his questions and the answers they had received, and of his own search and examination of the ship, he readily gave his own considered view of what had happened.

In James Winchester's view a rough sea had shifted the cargo. At least one barrel had been damaged sufficiently to release alcohol fumes that blew off the hatch cover after the pressure had built up. This happened not a great while before the *Dei Gratia* came up with the abandoned brigantine. He felt that the unrusted state of several razors left behind by the crew as well as some of their clothing hung up to dry supported this argument, and it was one with which Captain Moorhouse was in full agreement.

According to the Winchester explanation of what most likely happened, Captain Briggs, with a wife and small child aboard, became alarmed by the fumes rising from the hold with the blown hatch cover, and feared for the lives of all aboard and in his charge. He gave the order to abandon ship without loss of time, fearing a possible explosion in the hold and not knowing fully the actual amount of damage suffered by the cargo.

So the ship's boat was launched and stood off, its occupants expecting to see the ship they had left blown skywards, for there was a fire in the galley by which the cook heated meals, and at any moment the fumes might reach the galley.

However, no further explosion occurred, and when a breeze blew up and freshened Benjamin Briggs most likely decided that the fumes were being blown away, and had ordered his men to row back to the *Mary Celeste*.

Unfortunately the breeze continued to freshen, and the deserted brigantine had enough canvas on her rigging to ensure she moved smartly before it. The men in the small boat could not overtake her. Indeed, they had to row with a growing feeling of despair as the realization came to them that not only would they fail to reach their abandoned ship, but that the seas were rising under the whip of the wind, which at that time of the year would have been bitterly cold.

In the view of James Winchester the ten lives in the small boat had been lost when the men's strength gave out and the seas began to pound it without mercy.

This is the general agreement among responsible parties today. But even at the time that Winchester spoke, scores of incredible rumours and theories were being circulated both in Europe and North America. The story of possible mutiny was believed by many, although there was nothing known to support it save the rusty cutlass left on deck and some reported damage to the *Mary Celeste*'s bows. However, this last point was one that was argued hotly, for seamen who had gone aboard the *Mary Celeste* in Gibraltar had claimed the damage was no more than normal wear and tear due to port dockings and facing heavy seas. In short, the bow timbers had been strained, and from understandable hazards. They had not been damaged in a scuffle aboard.

Or even deliberately.

It was no less a person than the Queen's Advocate at Gibraltar, a gentleman of lively imagination named Flood, who suggested that the crew might have deliberately damaged the ship they were deserting to make her appear not worth salvaging—in short, a floating wreck that could be left to tide and time to finish off. Mr. Flood had a reason for saying this for he was involved with the terms of the claim for salvage. He did not approach the situation with an open mind. He was one who believed a drunken crew had got eager for blood and had murdered their mate and captain as well as the captain's wife and child. After throwing their victims overboard they had fled in the brigantine's only boat.

Not only was this general argument unsupported by anything of weight, but the marine surveyor at Gibraltar, who spent five hours and more examining the salvaged *Mary Celeste*, had neither claimed the cargo had been damaged on purpose nor charged that damage had been deliberately done to the ship.

Possibly the Queen's Advocate's sensational suggestion was in some measure responsible for an even more sensational suggestion that was made a short while after. This was to the effect that Benjamin Briggs was responsible for the mystery.

The captain of the *Mary Celeste*, it was suggested, had gone out of his mind. A madman had committed murder and mayhem aboard the ill-fated craft.

While this was certainly in the tradition of some of the best horror fiction of the period, it was, as a valid claim, so far-fetched as to be unbelievable. It was suggested that

Benjamin Briggs was a religious maniac—although he had never paraded himself as a particularly devout man. But he was said to have been overcome by a sudden determination to remove those he loved and those in his charge from the sinful snares of the world.

His mind deranged in this way, he had seized the cutlass that had been found and killed his wife and his little daughter. Stimulated by this fearful blood-letting, he had stalked his mate and the other members of the brigantine's crew. With the cunning of a homicidal maniac he had cut them down, one by one. Afterwards he had thrown the butchered bodies over the side. Finally his reason had returned, and he had launched the boat and set himself adrift, bent only on removing himself from a ship he had turned into a slaughter-house.

With this dreadful theory there was no attempt to explain how a madman had succeeded in defeating seven members of his crew, who might have been expected to notice the coming of insanity in their captain. Nor was the absence of fearful bloodstains explained.

Some people insisted that the unhappy murderer had thrown himself from the deck of his own ship. They did not stop to consider who, in that case, could have launched the missing boat.

The *Dei Gratia*'s first officer gave his own version of what could have happened, just as he had explained it to Captain Moorhouse after returning shaken from climbing aboard the deserted *Mary Celeste*.

To the more rational-minded at the court of inquiry it seemed then, as now, that the storm that had sent some of the barrels rolling around in the hold, and had damaged one sufficiently to make it leak, might have sprung a timber out of true; thus enough seawater could have been let in, while the waves were high, to collect to a depth of three feet. When the storm gave over, the gaping timber was squeezed back in place and no more seawater was shipped in calmer weather. Whether Captain Briggs gave the order to abandon ship because of the evidence of a leak, or because the hatch cover was blown off by alcohol fumes, or for possibly both these reasons, is still the point from which different opinions branch.

But whatever the captain's reason, it is certain that his crew were behaving in an orderly manner when they abandoned ship, and there is every likelihood that they were obeying their captain's command, given because he had the wellbeing of all aboard the *Mary Celeste* very much at heart. This would have been consistent with Benjamin Briggs' known character. He was a respected ships' captain and a mariner of great experience. He would not have acted in anything amounting to panic. He may have been urging haste, but he would have thought out his course of action and would have been taking it because it seemed to him the wisest and best to be taken in the circumstances as he understood them.

So the laden boat pulled away from a ship that was not doomed, leaving behind a mystery still debated as it has been from the time of the Gibraltar court of inquiry.

Perhaps it was to be expected that a number of people claiming to be survivors should turn up around the globe from time to time in the years following. These undoubted impostors were responsible for some of the more bizarre fables put in circulation about what happened that winter's day when the boat dropped over the *Mary Celeste*'s side, leaving the brigantine to drift into the path of the approaching *Dei Gratia*.

It is certain the small boat with any survivors was not to be seen through David Moorhouse's telescope or Benjamin Briggs' friend would have turned his ship around and sailed after it. Without first sighting that open boat it would have been futile to go seeking it with no clue to the direction in which it had gone. This despite the fact that the *Dei Gratia*'s captain had formed the firm opinion that the boat had left the *Mary Celeste* not very long before his first officer climbed aboard the deserted brigantine.

After James Winchester had taken possession of the *Mary Celeste* she was refitted and put back into the trade for which she had been built. She continued to ply the high seas, carrying cargoes up and down the Atlantic, for another thirteen years, until she piled up on Roshell's Reef, off the coast of Haiti, the voodoo island, on January 3rd, 1885.

When she sank under the Caribbean waves she left in nautical history a name associated with what is possibly the most famous of all mysteries of the sea.

4

The Incredible Affair of the Cock Lane Ghost

During the second half of the eighteenth century, a very strange mystery plagued the townsfolk living in central London.

Midway between Smithfield and Holborn is the road that has been known for hundreds of years as Cock Lane, which links Snow Hill and Giltspur Street. A few yards south, on the corner of Newgate Street, one can look across the road at the Old Bailey, built on the site of the former Newgate Prison.

This was the area of London that a little more than two hundred years ago first heard of the Cock Lane ghost and a mystery that was to set all London by the ears, fashionable and the so-called lower orders alike.

One can imagine the writer Samuel Johnson setting out one morning from his house in Gough Square, off Fleet Street, where he had five years before viewed the publication of his famous dictionary, and being greeted by a friend who asked him if he had heard of the mysterious doings in Cock Lane.

Johnson would have been interested for he was a Londoner by adoption, and the scandals, rumours, and news buzzing in London's streets all formed part of his mental diet. He would have chewed over the subject of the Cock Lane ghost with great relish even though he refused to digest it.

The mystery of what all London came to know as the Cock Lane ghost was really the mystery of the individual Smithfield and the surrounding area came to refer to as Scratching Fanny. The Cockney sense of humour was seldom more keen than when inventing nicknames, and Scratching Fanny, for a Cockney-bestowed nickname in the circumstances, was suitable, grim and yet fairly amusing.

The Fanny referred to was a woman calling herself Mrs. Fanny Kemp. Of the three titles Fanny was the only one to which she could truthfully lay claim. She wasn't married, and certainly not to the Mr. Kemp with whom she lived in a modest lodging in Cock Lane, for he was her brother-in-law. This irregular arrangement was maintained despite Fanny's readiness to find fault and to pick a quarrel at any time. She was a high-spirited young woman with a quick tongue, and when things displeased her she soon became vocal and shrill.

There must have been many occasions during the time the couple lived together in the Cock Lane lodging when the brother-in-law regretted setting up home with Fanny. Quite possibly his regret was shared by their landlord, a man named Parsons who did his best not to become involved in the disturbances created by Fanny's sharp temper and sharper tongue, but who more often than not failed. In short, there were times in Cock Lane when Fanny was a nuisance, and when she became ill and took to her bed there were not many sympathizers. However, Fanny's illness was more serious than at first supposed.

It was winter time, and January's snows hid some of the ugliness of the Smithfield district. The room where Fanny lay coughing and shivering was cold, but as her strength ebbed she lacked the will to complain. She was dying without anyone in the house realizing it. Indeed, her death came as a shock to her brother-in-law and to the Parsons family, which included a daughter of fourteen named Elizabeth, a strange child with quick darting eyes and secretive ways, who had not taken to Fanny.

After the local midwife, who usually had the task of laying out the bodies of the dead and making them presentable for burying, had visited the Kemp lodging arrangements were made for the dead woman to be provided with a coffin, which was to be removed to a vault beneath St. John's Church in Clerkenwell.

The woman who had called herself Mrs. Fanny Kemp went to what was thought to be her last resting place almost unaccompanied. The brother-in-law with whom she had lived, who was now generally looked upon as a widower, returned to Cock Lane, where for a time the only words spoken in the lodging were addressed by himself to himself. Not surprisingly he found living in the lodging that had known Fanny's lively presence far from comfortable, and as he was a man with no great liking for conversing with himself he decided to seek accommodation elsewhere.

He gave Parsons notice that he was leaving and duly packed his few possesions and removed them and himself. His going left the Parsons family with a problem. Should they relet the lodging or give the room where Fanny had died to their daughter Elizabeth, who was now too big to remain sleeping with other members of the family?

The pros and cons seemed evenly balanced in the mind of Elizabeth's father, but as he was not at that time being pressed for money he believed that his daughter should have the benefit of this happy state. Accordingly Elizabeth moved into the room that had been Fanny's bedchamber.

Not very long after this decision had been taken and the domestic sleeping arrangements altered, the family was wakened in the middle of a cold winter's night by strange tapping sounds. These sounds went on and stopped, only to continue later. The next morning the startled and bewildered family discussed this curious and totally unexpected event.

'They were scratching sounds,' insisted Mrs. Parsons, a woman who had enjoyed little sleep the past night.

'I'd call them knockings,' said her husband.

They discussed whether it was possible that they had imagined the sounds and decided no, for they had both heard them and very distinctly.

'They seemed to come from Elizabeth's room,' said the girl's mother. 'I'm sure of that.'

Her husband was not so sure, but agreed that the sounds had come from the part of the house where their daughter now slept. They agreed to say nothing about the night-time disturbances to friends or neighbours in Cock Lane.

'This is something best kept to ourselves,' said the husband, and his wife agreed.

'Especially as Elizabeth heard nothing,' she reminded him.

But that night the family's sleep was again disturbed, and on this occasion the noises were more distinctly scratching sounds.

'It must be a rat,' said the husband, wide awake and sitting up in bed.

'We've never had rats before,' his wife said, 'so I don't see why it should be a rat.'

'I'll go and see for myself,' she was told.

Parsons lit a candle and by the light of its dancing flame, with a chill draught reaching under the bottom of his long nightshirt, he made his way cautiously in the direction of the scratching sounds. He traced them to the room where his fourteen-year-old daughter slept on her own. He trod on a loose floorboard and after that there was no further scratching.

He retraced his way to his bed.

'Well, was it a rat?' his wife wanted to know.

The puzzled man climbed back between the sheets and dropped his head on his dented pillow.

'I can't say. It stopped suddenly. If it was a rat I frightened it away.'

'Well,' his wife insisted, 'I still say it was no rat. We have no rats in this house.'

They settled down to find sleep again, but no sooner had the husband started to snore than his wife was shaking him awake.

'The sounds have started again,' she said fearfully. 'Listen.'

The disturbed man again hauled himself up in the bed and sat listening. He heard the sounds, but they had changed in character. They were no longer scratchings, but more a series of thumps or knockings.

For the second time that night he rose from his bed and with his candle held high went in search of the sounds and their source. Again he arrived at Elizabeth's room only for the sounds to stop suddenly.

This time he had carefully avoided the loose floorboard.

He opened the door of his daughter's room and stood there shivering in the cold of the early hours, listening to the regular rhythm of the girl's breathing. He closed the door, went back to where his wife was waiting, and told her that without doubt the sounds had come from their daughter's room.

'What shall we do?' she asked.

'I don't know,' her worried husband confessed. 'But perhaps tomorrow night there will be no sounds.'

That proved to be a forlorn hope. The next night and on the following night the sounds were heard, scratchings and knockings which stopped only to start up again after an hour or two, so that the family did not get a reasonable night's sleep. By this time Parsons was a man becoming fearful of what the mysterious night sounds heard in his home might mean. They were not heard during the daytime, and it was in the daytime that a thorough search of Elizabeth's room was made. Nothing that could account for the strange noises was found.

The mysterious sounds continued.

So did the search for their origin. The floorboards in Elizabeth's room were removed and the joists below tested. None was loose and no rat dirts were found nor any sign of the floor's woodwork being gnawed by a rodent's teeth. The room was put back as it had been.

Only for the mysterious scratchings to return after nightfall and when the family had retired.

The next day all other movable sections of wood were removed in Elizabeth's room. Wainscoting and panels were prised away from the walls, revealing nothing to the puzzled gaze of the searchers. The wooden sections were nailed in place again, made secure.

That night the noises returned.

'I've had enough of this. Tomorrow we take Elizabeth out of that room,' her husband decided.

His wife agreed.

Accordingly the next day the change was made. Elizabeth, her bed, and her few belongings were taken from the room where Fanny had died and moved to another part of the house.

But this sensible move did not stop the mysterious noises that were making the nights hideous for Parsons and his thoroughly scared wife. As soon as they were falling asleep they were jerked wide awake by the return of those familiar but unexplained night sounds.

Again Parsons rose from his bed and tracked the sounds. They no longer came from the room in which Fanny had died. Instead, they came from a different part of the house. He again traced them to the room occupied by his daughter. Not only had the mysterious noises changed direction, but they had become much louder.

That night there was no sleep for the harassed husband and wife.

'The house is haunted,' the woman insisted.

Her husband did not contradict her.

The next morning she could contain the terrible news no longer. She unburdened herself to a neighbour with whom she had shared confidences in the past. Mary Jones believed in the supernatural.

She recalled that there had been some ill feeling between the dead Fanny and Elizabeth Parsons. She told the mother, 'I think Mrs. Kemp's ghost is returning each night.'

This startling suggestion prompted a request for advice about the best thing to do in the supernatural circumstances. Mary Jones didn't fail her neighbour.

'You must try to communicate with it,' she asserted in a tone of instant authority that is often heard today.

Parsons was consulted, and reluctantly he agreed. The best way of communication was discussed, and it was thought that the most direct way would be the best. When the sounds were next heard the ghost should be addressed and asked some very straight questions.

There was no delay in adopting this scheme, for that night the ghost sounds did not keep the excited listeners waiting. Parsons put the questions, which had been designed to secure fresh information. The responses of the unnatural visitant were to be one rap for yes and two for no – the ghost apparently agreeing to this system.

The responses to Parsons' questions proved undeniably startling. When he asked point-blank if Fanny had been murdered there was a sharp tap that unquestionably came from the room where Elizabeth Parsons was in bed.

With the keenness of someone who has invented a new and exciting game, Parsons went on to elaborate, asking questions in rapid order and receiving rapid taps and knocks in reply.

According to what the man and his wife told friends next morning, they were informed by the unearthly intruder into their home that Fanny had not only been murdered, but the murder was committed by Kemp. This had been achieved by dosing the sick woman with arsenic. In answer to another of Parsons' very leading questions the listeners in the pre-dawn period were informed how the arsenic had been mixed in a mug of purl, so that its taste would not be detected.

This last seemed very acceptable to Parsons and his wife, for Fanny had been at her shrillest after imbibing gin, and purl was a drink of hot beer or ale in which gin was mixed, a strong brew for a chilly January. There was a time when such a drink was known, with another touch of Cockney humour, as a dog's nose.

In all, the ghost had shown an almost human interest in gossip and small-talk on gruesome subjects, which somehow proved very reassuring to the landlord and his wife. Of course, Mary Jones had to be told of the result of following her suggestion. She was so pleased that she lost no time in proclaiming to other friends the value of her method of dealing with the ghost in the Parsons' house.

That began a rumour that refused to be halted and grew with each passing day.

'Have you heard about the ghost in Cock Lane?' was very soon an everyday greeting between friends who had not seen each other for some time.

In time that formula of greeting changed to 'Have you been to hear the ghost in Cock Lane?'

For suddenly and almost unaccountably London had a new craze—going to hear the Cock Lane ghost. This was made possible by Parsons suddenly discovering that he had both the nature and the talent of a successful showman. As soon as the news had spread beyond Cock Lane and Smithfield and the curious had started to arrive and stand gawking at the house, Parsons had allowed several to enter provided they paid for the privilege.

After that a flood of impulsive and curious persons made nightly descent on the Cock Lane area. They dropped coins into Parsons' ready palm and were allowed to enter and climb the stairs and listen to the rappings and thumpings. The nightly visitors were a strange mixture, for anyone who could raise the price of entry was welcomed by Parsons.

The ghost arrived promptly whenever payment had been made and did not apparently become overcome with the sheer boredom of visiting that drab house night after night.

In the daytime the ghost enjoyed rare publicity in both the taverns and the journals of the day. It became a fad of the year to go to Cock Lane. When the curtain rang down at Drury Lane or in the Haymarket coachmen were told to drive their carriages to Smithfield. High-spirited parties arrived straight from the play or the opera to hear the Cock Lane ghost and add to the riches of the Parsons family. There was a period when nightly it was impossible to drive through Smithfield because carriages of all kinds blocked the roads. From being the least fashionable end of London it came to be, for a rewarding period for Parsons, one of the most fashionable.

There was an air of what today we would call permissiveness about these odd gatherings of nobles and the notorious, the famous and the infamous, the fearful and the fearsome, of all sexes and all ages, healthy or infirm, and as a result a fresh site was chosen for finding similiar thrills.

Overspill crowds made their way to the crypt of St. John's Church in Clerkenwell, where some spent the entire night, and in daylight these pallid seekers of night-time excitement swore that they had heard scratchings from the coffin holding the remains of Fanny.

Instead of spoiling the mystery this double shift being worked by Scratching Fanny only made the visits more popular, more fashionable, and regretted by only one person—the landlord in Cock Lane who had no valid reason for collecting entrance fees in the crypt of a Clerkenwell church.

At the height of the Scratching Fanny craze, with the ghostly visitant working several double shifts nightly, authority decided it had to take notice of what was happening in the British capital. Kemp, who had been thoroughly aroused by the rumour of murder and arsenic and purl and his own villainy, had gone to a magistrate to display a signed death certificate which stated that Fanny had died of confluent smallpox. The magistrate might have been interested in a limited fashion, but not to the extent of satisfying the complainant by endeavouring to persuade hundreds of people nightly that they were making fools of themselves.

So Kemp remained a man believed by all London to be a villain. He was even ignored by the humanists and scientists with a mind for fashionable demonstrations. Fanny might have died of confluent smallpox and the ghost that answered questions with raps might have lied, but Elizabeth Parsons remained and as she was apparently the source of the mystery tests had to be carried out to further human knowledge.

Over the protests of her father, her hands and feet were tied and she was closely watched through the long nights.

The sounds continued to arrive.

Science was baffled, the humanists astonished. But these fresh searchers did not give up easily, and what they did was full of news value and kept the crowds coming. Some

. . . her hands and feet were tied and she was closely watched . . .

inventive genius had the fourteen-year-old girl hung up in a hammock slung from ceiling rafters. Her hands and feet were projected over the hammock 'as far as might be,' in the phrase used by one observer. They were then bound so that they could not be withdrawn.

Elizabeth Parsons was kept in this uncomfortable state for seventy-two hours—three whole nights as well as three days. Anyone who treated a child in this barbarous fashion today would be either jailed or put in a mental home.

Elizabeth's discomfort, however, produced a change that seemed to prove her torturers' case. During the nights she hung in her hammock there were no tappings in her room. The ghost apparently sulked or went on strike or gave a grudging silence as a sign of displeasure at this treatment of the girl.

But the tormentors of Elizabeth immediately claimed they had solved the mystery. The girl had been making the 'supernatural' sounds.

Elizabeth burst into tears and denied the charges. She was joined by her father, now fearful that his private viewing would become out of favour and the flow of coins into his ready palm would stop.

The distressed and frightened girl was put back into her own bed the next night. Those who were responsible for the hammock experiment remained in the house, unwelcome guests her father was too scared to turn away. Sure enough, the scratchings and tappings and thumps started up again.

The Cock Lane ghost was back on the job.

But the novelty was over. Now it had been proved that if Elizabeth was out of her room the sounds ceased she found herself confronted by angry accusers who threatened her with dire punishment unless she confessed that she had been making the noises and fooling everyone who listened.

'Confess, girl,' she was urged.

Elizabeth burst into more tears. This was taken by some as a confession of sorts. They insisted that the girl should be searched.

'The sounds come from her body,' one claimed.

Another pointed out that the sounds of the past night had not been so noisy as on the many nights previous to the hammock experiment. That was considered to point even more firmly to her guilt for some unexplained reason.

Parsons held out as long as he could against giving way to these inquirers after the truth. Too much was being written and published for him to appear relucant for the truth to be discovered—if that were possible. He had taken too many fees from the stream of visitors to his home to risk being labelled a fraud who did not dare to court exposure. His wife was almost out of her senses. His neighbours were suddenly hostile. More than that, the popularity of his nightly show showed grave signs of being over.

The Cock Lane ghost was amazingly out of fashion and London waited for the outcome of this inquiry on the scene of the mysterious night noises.

So grudgingly Parsons gave way.

'Very well, you may search my daughter, but her mother and another matron must be present.'

This condition was agreed to, and the girl was helped out of her dress. When she stood in her underclothes she moved and a curious creak was heard. It seemed to come from the ribs of her stays, which in the manner of the time were held moulded to the figure by long laces or draw-strings.

When this adult garment was removed from the childish body a small thin piece of board fell from it. This piece of wood was said to be sufficient to have made the noises heard the previous night.

'This is the proof we sought,' the thoroughly alarmed

father was told. 'It has all been a shameful trick and will be dealt with by the law.'

However, if the examiners of Elizabeth Parsons thought their discovery would mean they would be hailed as heroes they were sadly out in their reckoning of Cockney humour. When their findings were published the whole of London burst into laughter, directed not least at the determined seekers of the truth.

The Cock Lane ghost had become a girl with a piece of board in her corsets.

It was the biggest joke of that winter.

The joke was discussed in alehouses and fashionable clubs. Everyone in fashionable London wanted to be a victim of the incredible trick. The best tellers of tales were soon entertaining their friends with the experiences they had undergone while visiting the house in Cock Lane.

It was a topic of mirth and caused much merriment to all except the now discredited Cock Lane landlord and his unhappy family, who were pointed to as figures of fun by neighbours and jeered at when they stepped abroad.

Fashion, as philosophers have taken pains to point out in almost every age that has dared to look itself in the face, is like a fickle woman.

After smiling on Parsons she now frowned and the change was like passing out of hot sunshine into frost. London continued enjoying its laughter directed at itself, little caring about the Parsons family's misfortunes, and they were sharp in the extreme.

A charge had been laid against them and they were tried with several friends who, too late, regretted having helped Parsons control the crowd of visitors. They were found guilty of imposing a grave fraud on the public and were sentenced to terms of imprisonment.

When this last act in the mystery drama of Scratching Fanny was reported in the journals the laughter was stilled.

While there were many who felt that the family deserved to be punished, there were some who thought they should be praised for giving London its biggest joke for a long time, but these were not taken seriously.

On the other hand, there were some who doubted whether the Parsons family had truly been guilty of fraud and whether they had rightfully been punished. Some of these doubters began penning letters to the journals. In this way there began a vast and continuing debate as to the genuine explanation of the so-called Cock Lane ghost. It has continued into the present century, when psychic researchers have tried to find good reason for the belief that Scratching Fanny was no fraud but a spirit working through the mediumship of Elizabeth Parsons.

There was a time, not long after the unhappy Parsons family had left Cock Lane for prison, when the argument became so bitter that several well-known personages came to blows over their inability to see eye to eye about the guilt or otherwise of Elizabeth Parsons. In later years writers found time to devote whole books to the subject, but that was after another strange event had taken place, not in Cock Lane, but in the crypt of St. John's Church.

It was decided at a time when the Cock Lane ghost had become a myth surrounded by a thin veil of clinging mystery to have the crypt cleared. This entailed removing many of the vaults and their contents. A number of the coffins were opened, and one of these was that containing the last remains of the woman who had called herself Mrs. Fanny Kemp, but had for two months after her death been known as Scratching Fanny.

The contents of her coffin surprised those who opened it, for her face and figure were seemingly well preserved and her features would certainly have been recognizable to anyone who had known her in life. Furthermore, her hair remained attached to her scalp.

'It's as though she's been preserved in some strange fashion,' one of the viewers peering into the opened coffin exclaimed in evident surprise. 'How can this be if she died of confluent smallpox?'

That was a very good question, and one that seemed to require an answer, for the disease recorded on the death certificate produced by Kemp would have begun a rapid decomposition of the woman's body before she was actually dead.

If she had died of that disease the contents of the coffin should have been almost liquid.

The coffin was closed and sent to a group of doctors, who made tests to the limit of their knowledge at that time, which was before James Marsh first published his famous test for the presence of arsenic in the *Edinburgh Philosophical Journal* of October 1836. They signed a statement that death could not have been caused by the ravages of confluent smallpox, which would have destroyed the body utterly, but it might have been caused by arsenic, which was known to preserve body tissue.

This was sufficient reason to begin the old argument again. According to Parsons the séance-like tappings had agreed to murder by arsenic, despite what was written on the death certificate produced by Kemp. How then could this curious contradiction, now supported by medical evidence, be supported?

Had Parsons shared a secret with Kemp or had he kept to himself a secret concerning murder in which Kemp had not shared? Whatever the answer, it seems conclusive that Fanny, one-time the biggest joke in London as she lay in her coffin, did die of arsenical poisoning. But who administered it and was it indeed given to her in a mug of purl?

If the Cock Lane ghost was explained by the piece of board concealed in Elizabeth's stays, and there are still doubters, there has been no conclusive evidence as to who helped Fanny into the next world with doses of a deadly poison.

One thing is certain.

Fanny did not poison herself, and just possibly she might not have been poisoned had she not had a weakness for a mug of purl.

5

Bad Blood on the *Bounty*

The story of the *Bounty*, a modest ship of two hundred and fifty tons, is the story of Captain William Bligh and the mutiny he provoked. Contained within that story, which has been a popular one for almost two hundred years, is the mystery of why there was bad blood between the ship's captain and the man whom Bligh had personally raised to the rank of master's mate.

Why did the *Bounty*'s master's mate, whose name was Fletcher Christian, hate his captain? Enough, in any case, to lead the mutiny that was to give Bligh the opportunity to demonstrate for all time his worth as a seaman. Enough, also, for Christian to set his captain adrift in an open boat in the confident belief that William Bligh would never reach a port where he could report the mutiny and Christian's part in it.

One thing is very certain. William Bligh misjudged Christian as much as the master's mate misjudged his captain.

History, possibly because of the fact that a mutiny occurred, has tended to do its own misjudging in the story, certainly of William Bligh. He was considered to be a harsh tyrant. He was not. He was a firm naval officer of his day who took no nonsense from those under him. He ordered no more floggings than any other captain of a ship in the late eighteenth century. But the floggings he ordered have been remembered, whereas those ordered by other naval captains have been forgotten.

Strangely, it was Bligh himself who made sure that the floggings he ordered when in command of the *Bounty* should not be forgotten. He made a point of relating them personally when giving evidence to an admiralty court. He never felt they were other than merited by the shipboard standards of his time.

Although most people today think only of Bligh as the strict captain in command of the *Bounty*, he had a very distinguished career in the Royal Navy. He was born in Plymouth on September 9th, 1754, of a family with Cornish roots. He had no rich relatives to help him start as a midshipman. He joined the Royal Navy as an able-bodied seaman when he was sixteen and first served aboard a ten-gun sloop, the *Hunter*. He remained with his first ship for little more than a year. He was studious and painstaking and must have created a good impression in circles where he was unknown personally, for Captain James Cook looking for a master to handle his ship the *Resolution* on his third voyage in her, which was to be the famous explorer's last, surprised everyone at the Admiralty by choosing William Bligh. Why Cook should have chosen Bligh is a minor mystery concerning the characters of the two men. But Cook was rarely at fault when handling men under his command. He must have seen a value in Bligh that was not so readily apparent to other commanders. This is all the more surprising when one realizes that, until Bligh had been chosen by him, Cook had never met his choice.

Cook may have been influenced by the fact that Bligh had become a specialist in the Royal Navy in two important subjects to an explorer, hydrography (study of the sea, its tides, etc.), and navigation. Moreover, Cook would certainly have been looking for a junior officer of promise who had a strong sense of discipline, for his third voyage was planned to take him in search of the mysterious North-west Passage, sought since Elizabethan times by British sea captains, and then back to the South Seas for further exploration. The voyage would take at least four years, and it is noteworthy that when the American President heard of it he gave orders that commanders of ships in the new American Navy should not interfere with or bring to action Cook's valiant *Resolution*, in which he had already discovered the vast continent of Australia.

Four years away from home would try the courage and discipline of all aboard Cook's ship. So Bligh's appeal as a recognized disciplinarian was a factor that recommended him strongly to his new commander. Cook's murder by some treacherous natives in the Sandwich Islands, known today as Hawaii, the fiftieth State in the American union, has robbed us of the famous explorer's verdict on William Bligh. One cannot but feel it might have offset most of the harsh criticisms made by later ages that depended too much on a one-sided view of the *Bounty* mutiny.

For Bligh that four years in the *Resolution* was the true turning point in a lengthy career. Because of his experience gained both north and south of the equator he not only perfected his navigational and naval skills, but learned how to control men placed under him and to ensure that they remained physically fit and in good health during long spells away from land.

James Cook was the pattern by which Bligh tried to shape his own career. The influence of the famous explorer on him cannot be over-stressed.

When at last the *Resolution* returned to England Bligh was granted a thousand pounds for his contribution to the official account of the voyage. A short while afterwards he married Elizabeth Betham, who came of a seafaring family and was the niece of a man who had his own fleet of trading vessels. Moreover, this uncle had a cousin, Vice-Admiral John Campbell, who was in a position to help Bligh receive the command of the *Britannia*. Thus the boy who had started his naval career in the lower deck found himself Lieutenant Bligh with his own command.

One of the *Britannia*'s company was a certain Fletcher Christian, the son of a Manx lawyer. When Bligh, following the example of James Cook, set himself to win his crew's approval by kindness and consideration, he extended special favours to young Christian. He personally undertook to instruct the lawyer's son in navigation and in cartography (map-making). The two men got on well together, and their liking for each other was mutual. So much so that Christian went out of his way to record Bligh's courtesy and friendship after the *Britannia* had completed her voyage. In the same spirit of friendship and appreciation, Bligh made a special recommendation of Fletcher Christian's seamanship and resources to the Admiralty.

Yet these were the two men who were a few years later to turn their happy relationship with each other completely upside-down, and their suddenly developed hatred for one another was to make the *Bounty*'s notorious mutiny not only possible, but a violent confrontation that neither could avoid.

The *Bounty* was another naval ship chosen for a special task. It was decided to send her to the South Seas to gather specimen plants of the breadfruit tree. The plants were to be carefully cared for and nurtured throughout a lengthy return journey, for they were designed to be transplanted in soil to the West Indies, where their fruit would provide part of a staple diet for slaves working on West Indian plantations.

The men most eager for this experiment to be made were merchants in the City of London who had invested large sums in those plantations in the New World. To ensure that the Admiralty would not stand in their way, the City merchants had found a way to interest King George the Third in the intended experiment, and had received royal support for the employment of a naval vessel. Indeed the merchants' royal patron was sufficiently interested to ask that some of the plants brought by the *Bounty* from the South Seas should be sent to Kew Gardens.

So the *Bounty* was made ready for a lengthy voyage and command of her was given to Lieutenant William Bligh. Before the *Bounty* sailed the Royal Society decided to offer a gold medal to anyone who could succeed in keeping the plants alive until they reached their destination. The procedure was to be to take aboard young plants of the breadfruit tree at Tahiti and to transport them successfully to both Jamaica and St. Vincent, in the West Indies, as these islands were almost in the same latitude.

William Bligh, with his knowledge of the seas through which he was expected to sail the *Bounty*, could be forgiven for seeing the outcome of the *Bounty*'s voyage as a personal triumph well within his grasp, and he was in no way displeased at the thought of receiving the Royal Society's gold medal.

In the event he was to be sadly disappointed and to return to England not only empty-handed, but without the *Bounty* – largely because he chose as the *Bounty*'s master's mate that same Fletcher Christian to whom he had shown favour in the recent past.

The *Bounty* upanchored two days before Christmas in 1787, and the crew might be forgiven for considering that they had been cheated of Christmas ashore. If this left them unhappy the weather into which the *Bounty* sailed after clearing the mouth of the Thames could have left them with a feeling of deep depression. It was foul in the extreme. The huge waves of the English Channel tossed the *Bounty* from trough to crest and back again as though the craft were merely an over-large cork.

Bligh, perhaps sensing the mood of his company and wishing to raise their low spirits, made changes from the accepted routine as soon as the *Bounty* sailed into calmer weather. He decided the men could have a full eight hours below decks in the wintry weather, instead of the normal four, by the creation of three watches. He further went out of his way to show favour to his master's mate by appointing him acting lieutenant, which made Christian of higher rank than the master, a man whose name was Fryer.

Fryer may certainly have considered himself to have reason for feeling unhappy at this treatment by his commander, but that could hardly apply to Fletcher Christian. Bligh kept a tidy ship and his men were worked to maintain good discipline and order in the company. But the man who has been labelled by some as a cruel bully did not order the first flogging for disobedience until the seventh week out from England. No one could claim Bligh was in a hurry to inflict pain he was supposed to enjoy giving to others.

However, the battering taken by the *Bounty* forced Bligh to put into Tenerife for repairs. Such a neccessity in winter could not have been viewed as a good omen for the enterprise, which required the *Bounty* to sail round the Horn to Tahiti, or Otaheite as the island was spelled on the charts of two hundred years ago.

The fierce Channel storms had washed overboard some of the ship's stores, including food supplies. In Tenerife Bligh urged the early completion of repairs, but he refused to wait additional time to add to his low food stocks. As a result, when the *Bounty* sailed from Tenerife she had a shortage of flour, and Bligh ordered that the bread allowance should be cut by a third.

It was this enforced bread rationing that created the first rumblings of discontent. The rumblings became clearer when the captain paraded his ship and pronounced himself dissatisfied by the crew's notions of personal hygiene and shipboard cleanliness. He ordered the men to work in off-duty hours, scrubbing decks and shirts alike. It seemed that what William Bligh could give with one hand he could take back with the other.

No onc has ever earned friendship or praise for such a practice, and Captain Bligh was no exception.

One person aboard the *Bounty* who might have had doubts at this stage was the man to whom it was all new, from seasickness to weevily biscuits. This was David Nelson, a naturalist and horticulturist who had been entrusted by Sir Joseph Banks, the scientific adviser to the Royal Botanical Gardens at Kew, with the task of selecting the most suitable breadfruit trees on Tahiti for transplanting in the West Indies.

For Nelson it was to prove a tragic voyage. The botanist who was numbered among the keenest of Banks' humorously dubbed plant hunters was to prove a loyal supporter of Bligh in the hour of reckoning, but his loyalty cost him dearly later on. So far as is known there was no warm friendship between Bligh and his most important passenger, but it can be assumed that the two men, of very different temperaments, found areas of agreement and even interest in which they could find each other's company rewarding.

When the *Bounty* was some two and a half months out from England Bligh made a significant entry in his daily journal. On that day in March 1788 he wrote in his cramped hand that he had 'found it necessary to punish Mathew Quintal with two dozen lashes for insolence and mutinous behaviour.' He added a note of almost equal significance, 'Before this I had not occasion to punish any person aboard.'

But it is certain that Bligh's order for the cat-o' nine-tails to be laid across Quintal's back not only gave rise to fresh muttering below decks, but was a painful shipboard lesson for the curious landlubber David Nelson. It was from this time that Bligh's temper shortened noticeably. He was certainly a man who was sorely tried by the elements. After the dirty weather at the start of his voyage, he crossed the Atlantic only to run into a series of blizzards at Cape Horn. The *Bounty* ran through a blinding curtain of snow. Bligh spared neither himself nor his crew. With them he worked long hours while the rigging froze and the decks became encased in a sheet of ice. The action of storm and ice tore some of the little ship's timbers from their caulking and Bligh faced the threat of his craft becoming a sadly leaking tub.

Perhaps another captain might have turned back and waited for the bad weather to blow itself out. Not William Bligh. Any hazard of the sea was to be overcome. He saw that as a mission to be accomplished.

So the *Bounty* fought the freezing Cape Horn storms for a month. During that time life aboard became a dreary existence in which everyone forgot the meaning of leisure and comfort. Night and day the ship had to be fought through mounting seas that threatened to sink her. It must have been a particularly miserable spell of days for the botanist on his way to a sunny clime.

But at the end of that grim month Bligh had to face a stark reality that did nothing to lighten his mood or lessen his temper. He had lost his fight against the elements. To continue would be foolhardy and would put his ship at serious risk. The man who had fought Cape Horn and its weather untiringly suddenly gave in to what he now saw as the inevitable. He had been beaten. His ship leaked, his crew were exhausted, and to continue would mean the small ship's foundering. He took defeat badly, but the *Bounty* turned tail and ran for the Cape of Good Hope.

Those were bad days for anyone aboard the *Bounty* to have to live through. This was the period when William Bligh became a changed man, when he and Fletcher Christian became distant from one another. However, precisely what brought about that change in Bligh towards his master's mate and in Christian towards his commander still remains a mystery. This was when their friendship changed to bitter enmity, when former favours were forgotten and earlier feelings of appreciation were crushed by feelings of dislike.

The *Bounty* dropped anchor at the Cape on May 23rd, and Bligh went ashore to arrange for further repairs to be done to his leaking ship. The work took a month, during which time the crew rested and brooded on their grievances. Unquestionably that was a sad month for William Bligh. Had his men been cheerful, with full bellies and plenty of work to occupy them in sunlit days, the outcome of that fateful voyage might have been very different.

Christian found himself closer to the idle members of the crew than to the captain who shut himself up in his cabin and brooded on what ill-chance had done to his ship and himself. While Christian felt a new sympathy with men whose ill-humour reflected his own mood in those days at anchor, Bligh sank more into a shipboard isolation that was later to make it difficult for him to recover the respect of those who had to take his orders.

But at last the *Bounty* was seaworthy again and supplied with a fresh stock of provisions, and Bligh decided to leave the Cape and head for Tasmania, an island to be found on his charts against the name Van Diemen's Land. The *Bounty* was two months on that crossing of the southern seas, and it was on August 20th that Bligh and his ship arrived off Tasmania. David Nelson began to take a fresh interest in life.

Two months later the botanist was possibly the only really happy man aboard the *Bounty*.

The reason was that Bligh arrived at Tahiti on the 25th of October. Nelson could look forward to selecting his plants and stowing them in the *Bounty*'s hold. He had been away from England for ten months, which had seemed far longer to him than to the sailors of the crew. Bligh had sailed in that time across twenty-seven thousand miles of ocean, much of it rough.

Why he decided on a long stay is another part of the mystery that helped to produce bad blood aboard his ship. An island chief named Tinah, informed of the reason for the *Bounty*'s anchoring off the island, informed Bligh that he could have as many plants of the breadfruit tree as he wished to take away. Bligh could have taken the chief at his word and quickly been off.

Instead, he remained at anchor for six months.

It was undoubtedly during that unexplained stay of half a year that the seeds of the notorious mutiny were sown aboard the *Bounty*. The men had little to do after attending to normal shipboard repairs except while away the tropic days in one another's company. They had ample time in which to air supposed grievances and blow them up into imagined wrongs. An attitude of conspiracy developed among the crew. It is possible that some of the men turned to Fletcher Christian because he lent a ready ear to their grumbling. In this case it is likely that Bligh became distrustful of the man he had favoured, and Christian, becoming aware of this, allowed resentment against his captain to sour his judgment of the man as distinct from the commander of the *Bounty*.

The truth of how the relationship between the two men changed has puzzled all students of the *Bounty* story, and cannot be explained even now, for if William Bligh had a right to expect loyalty and aid from any man aboard his ship that man was Fletcher Christian.

Morale among the *Bounty*'s crew sank to a low level for a number of reasons. Not only was there resentment on account of the long stay and against punishment ordered when discipline became dangerously slack aboard a ship of the Royal Navy, but thieves began using their light fingers. To Bligh this was unforgivable. If he was approached by a worried David Nelson about things that the botanist had observed, then he would have been even more determined to restore discipline on his ship. Certainly he was no longer reluctant to order floggings, as he had been when the voyage began.

During those tropic days off Tahiti William Bligh changed from a reasonably tolerant commander to one who became loathed by many of his crew, who came to consider him a tyrant.

The worsening relationship with Fletcher Christian could have played its part in this noticeable change. Bligh too was recalling incidents that had soured his thoughts about a crew who, in their captain's opinion, had a full complement of rogues among them.

Two incidents are notable. The first concerns the *Bounty*'s store of cheese. It is a story that has gained notoriety with the passage of time, for it has two versions, the crew's and the captain's.

According to the first, Bligh accused thieves of taking two cheeses from the cask in which they were kept. The cooper in charge of the cask maintained that the missing cheeses had been taken to the captain's table earlier on his instructions. Instead of accepting this explanation Bligh cut the crew's cheese allowance.

Bligh's own account is very different. According to him, the cheese cask was opened on deck when he wished to discover if the hot weather had caused the stored cheeses to deteriorate to the point of being uneatable. All the examined cheeses were found edible, and were put back in the cask, but later two were stolen and Bligh considered this the result of a conspiracy involving a good number of the crew. As no one owned up to the theft he stopped the crew's cheese ration.

Was the cooper the culprit? This was never discovered. But the man had a deep-seated grudge against Bligh for having him flogged for insubordination.

This atmosphere of worsening relations with his company extended beyond the crew involving the master, Fryer. One day when Bligh ordered Fryer to sign the ship's accounts he was met with a blunt refusal until Bligh had signed another document produced by the master. This was no less than a statement declaring that to date Fryer had done nothing to displease his commander. Bligh angrily refused to put his name to the document and gave Fryer a sharp dressing down, even reading to him a piece of naval law contained in the articles of war which he considered applied to the master.

So that man who had reason to resent Bligh's previous favouring of Christian now had even sharper reason to feel hostile towards his captain. Could Christian have smoothed things over and neglected to do so? It is possible. But if so, what were Christian's reasons?

Without satisfactory answers to such questions, one can only consider the known actions of the crew members. Two are helpful. The first concerned some of the crew who had put their heads together and decided to desert. They stole some food and eight muskets with ammunition, which were loaded into a cutter. They waited for a cloudy night with no moon and then they left the *Bounty* and sailed around the island until they found a small cove, where they beached the cutter, concealed it as best they could, and made their way inland. As an enterprise it was badly thought out and just as badly executed. Bligh found the cutter and men missing and asked for Tinah's help. His men soon came upon the cutter, which was returned to the *Bounty*, and then the island was scoured for the deserters. They too were found by Tinah's men and returned to their ship. Bligh assembled the entire company of the *Bounty* and had the deserters flogged publicly. Tinah and his men were given gifts for their aid.

But when the *Bounty*'s mooring hawser was almost severed the culprit was not discovered. This so affected Bligh that he almost quarrelled with Tinah about the incident.

Even Bligh realized at length that his stay was becoming too lengthy. He made up his mind to sail as soon as he could make his ship ready. The lazy life was over. The men who were about to become sailors again instead of beach-combers were freshly resentful at this new decision by their captain. Bligh didn't realize it. He had reached the point where he could do nothing that would earn the approval of the men under him. Christian could have helped to change this unfortunate state of affairs aboard the *Bounty*. He did nothing except listen to the men's grumbling and remain silent.

He was a man biding his own time for action. But again what had brought him to this personal crossroads is something that cannot be satisfactorily explained.

On April 4th, 1789, the *Bounty*'s anchors were drawn inboard and a sullen crew shook out the sails as the ship stood out to sea, watched by the assembled islanders on the white shore. Bligh paced his quarterdeck with a heavy frown. He had allowed Nelson to stow fifteen hundred breadfruit plants in one part of the ship for transplanting in the West Indies. Between decks there were twenty-four boxes and thirty-nine tubs with growing breadfruit trees that had been transplanted in Tahiti soil. There were also 774 pots with all kinds of growing plants from the island. The *Bounty* left Tahiti as a veritable floating horticultural nursery.

He had also informed his crew that everything aboard belonged to the captain. To the sullen men who had to sail the ship these might have sounded as mere empty words. But when Bligh added that he was entitled to nine-tenths of each man's personal possessions these words had sudden and sharp meaning.

Bligh was probably referring to the goods and gear the men had collected on the island during the six months' stay. The men thought otherwise.

Again Christian might have helped to explain things, even though Fryer refused to stand by his captain. But once more Fletcher Christian remained puzzlingly silent. On the nineteenth day after leaving Tahiti it was Christian's turn to earn Bligh's sharply voiced displeasure.

The *Bounty* was making for the island of Annamooka, and Bligh gave orders that when the island was reached no member of the crew should resort to the use of firearms if the natives attacked them, and not unnaturally the men protested. This time Christian was not silent. He sided with the men and echoed their protest. Bligh responded bitterly to what he considered an act of treachery. Four days later he became obsessed about some coconuts he accused Christian of stealing.

Christian denied taking the coconuts, but Bligh did not believe him. Before members of the crew he told Christian he would make the master's mate glad to jump overboard. This was the same as saying he would make the other man glad to commit suicide.

Undoubtedly, in the dangerous atmosphere aboard, this was going too far. Christian told Cole the boatswain that he was tired of being treated like a dog. He had a mind to make a raft and set sail to Tahiti again. Cole tried to discourage him. Next Christian told the carpenter, Purcell, of his plan, and also two young midshipmen, Steward and Hayward, who agreed to help him. The raft was made and provisions for it were hidden in the hammock of the ship's boy, Bob Tinkler, before Fletcher Christian had second thoughts about this piece of folly, which could end with the deserters losing their lives.

Lying awake at night thinking over the plan, Christian decided the best scheme would be to seize the ship and then set the captain adrift. When daylight came he sounded out the crew, and found seven who were prepared to become mutineers. Three of them had been flogged. Mathew Quintal was one of them. Joe Coleman, the ship's armourer, allowed them to have the key to the arms chest when he was told a cruising shark had to be shot. The mutineers armed themselves. Cutlass in hand, Fletcher Christian led them to Bligh's cabin, where the captain was found in his nightshirt. Christian ordered him on deck.

It was Bligh's first confrontation with a man who had now announced that he was his enemy. For Bligh it must be said that he refused to back down before armed might or the threat of death he saw in the faces of desperate men. 'I refuse to leave this cabin not in uniform,' he told the mutineers.

At that moment Christian was too new to mutiny to order his followers to manhandle the captive Bligh, who was grudingly allowed to dress, then had his hands tied behind his back and was taken to stand by the ship's mizzen mast.

Under Christian's orders a boat was lowered, and four men, including officers, were told to get into it. Bligh spoke up, demanding to know the mutiny leader's intentions, and was told by Christian, 'Hold your tongue, sir, or you are dead this instant.' Bligh was threatened with a bayonet.

Food and some navigational instruments were stowed in the boat. Then those Christian didn't trust to follow him were forced into the boat with the officers. Bligh was the last to be told to leave the *Bounty*.

'Will you set us adrift without arms?' asked the captain whose ship had been taken from him.

'Hold your tongue, sir,' said Christian, 'or you are dead this instant.'

This seemed to be a good joke to the men to whom Bligh had earlier refused arms. But when they laughed there was the strong odour of rum on their breath. Christian had taken the precaution of serving ample tots of rum to give his apprentice mutineers Dutch courage to commit a naval crime which could earn them a hanging if they were caught and brought to trial.

The bobbing boat with its cargo of castaways was cut loose. The mutineers lining the deck and laughing at their victims saw them as men going to their death. Four cutlasses were tossed into the boat and some old pieces of clothing.

Before the boat drifted out of earshot Bligh made an effort to come to terms with Fletcher Christian, a man whose hate he felt like hot metal that had touched his flesh, but without understanding. Bligh was thinking of the men ordered to keep him company on what was considered by the mutineers to be a death voyage, particularly of David Nelson, parted from his tropical plants and a victim of heavy despair as he crouched in the open boat.

'I'll pawn my honour,' Bligh called, 'I'll give my bond, Mr. Christian, never to think of this if you desist.'

It was a moment when he was supreme, a defeated man who still wore a mantle of awe as though it were a toga.

But Fletcher Christian was a man who had taken several steps too many to allow of retreat.

'No, Captain Bligh,' he shouted at the figure standing upright in the bobbing boat. 'If you had any honour things had not come to this, and if you had any regard for your wife and family you should have thought on them before and not behaved so much like a villain.'

They were the last words spoken between the two men whose basic characters made possible one of the most famous mutinies of all time. The story of how Bligh, finding fulfilment in hardship, both as man and seaman, finally brought his crew of castaways to safety against all the hazards of weather and sea and unfriendly natives on islands where the boat called is a saga of the sea that is an incredible escape story without parallel. It is also without mystery.

The mystery of the bad blood that created the mutiny on the *Bounty* was past satisfactory solution when Fletcher Christian refused Bligh's final offer to forget the mutiny if the mutineers returned to their duties and laid down their arms.

It was on the 28th April that Bligh and his castaways were set adrift. On March 19th, 1790, he arrived back in England. He had navigated 3,600 miles in an open boat in six weeks to reach Timor, in the East Indies, discovering the Fiji Islands on the way. One of Bligh's companions who did not complete the journey to England was David Nelson. He was alive when the open boat reached Timor, but died later and was afforded a funeral with full military honours.

After receiving the personal congratulations of King George the Third, the royal patron of the ill-fated *Bounty*'s voyage, Bligh attended the court-martial, where the decision was taken to send another ship of the Royal Navy to seize the now notorious mutineers. The frigate *Pandora* sailed for Tahiti. Only a few mutineers were found on the island, the rest having left with Fletcher Christian in the *Bounty*, accompanied by some native women from Tahiti. They reached the lonely island of Pitcairn, well off the trade routes, where for years they were lost to the world until found in the next century.

The captured mutineers were tried. Of the ten facing the court, four were acquitted and six sentenced to hang, but three of the doomed men were reprieved. The other three, Burkitt, Millward, and Ellison, were hanged from H.M.S. *Brunswick*'s yardarm on September 29th.

As for Bligh, promoted to post-captain, he took the *Providence* to Tahiti in 1791 and successfully transplanted breadfruit tree plants to the West Indies, so completing his mission in the *Bounty* which the mutiny interrupted. The breadfruit transplanting was a success and in 1794 William Bligh received the Royal Society's Gold Medal in recognition of his services.

He was commended by Nelson for the part he played in the naval action off Copenhagen, but when he arrived in Australia as the newly appointed Governor of New South Wales he proved a dismal failure as a colonial administrator. He returned to London and finished his eventful career as a Vice-Admiral of the Blue.

6

The Man who stole the Crown Jewels

Three living creatures could create an enthusiastic liking for them on the part of Charles the Second—a pretty woman who knew how to smile seductively, a racehorse with the lines of a thoroughbred that could win races, and a charming rogue whose manner could be entertaining.

Thomas Blood fell into the third category.

He was of Irish descent and was generally supposed to have been born in the Emerald Isle, and there is reason for believing the year might have been 1618. What is known is that he was the son of a prosperous blacksmith who by steady application and hard work, allied to an ability for shrewd bargaining, acquired a successful ironworks. An ironworks that could turn out forged steel could not help but be prosperous in an age when warring armies were bent on soaking the land with blood. Thomas had no liking for a smith's trade when he could be wearing breastplate and helmet and wielding a sword. When the Civil War broke out he joined the Parliamentary army.

He must have been a good soldier, for by the time Cromwell had emerged as victor and dictator and England was under military rule, Thomas Blood held a colonel's commission. When Cromwell sent his Ironsides to subdue the Irish Thomas Blood accompanied them. If he had any feeling for his compatriots at this time it was one of enmity. He not only killed Irishmen, he helped to conquer those who remained alive. He was one of those keen destroyers of his fellows who made the curse of Cromwell the most dreaded oath in the land. In fact, he played his part so well that the Lord Protector's second son, Henry, who had been made lord deputy in Ireland, singled him out for special favours, including titles to some estates forfeited by followers of the Stuart cause.

At the time of Oliver Cromwell's death, Colonel Blood was riding the crest of fortune's wave. He had accumulated, as an adventurer backing the winning side in the Civil War, land and status and an income of five hundred pounds per annum.

The Restoration was a disaster for Thomas Blood. He lost everything he had gained, lands, status, and money. Almost overnight he was ruined.

He took this about-face in his circumstances very badly. Temperamentally he was a rebel, and he had been one for far too long to assume the cloak of conformity. By upbringing as by persuasion, he was noncomformist. Actually a Presbyterian, although he was by no means a rigid sectarian, he was labelled a 'sectary' by the Stuart followers who sprang back into power and favour. The term not only meant he belonged to a sect in opposition to the returned king, but defined him as a dangerous opponent in himself. Thomas Blood lived up to his new label.

After a period of remaining quiet and undemonstrative, and most likely living from hand to mouth and finding little liking for the change, he again became an active rebel. He and others like him deemed the time had come in 1663 for an uprising in Ireland against the power of the Duke of Ormonde, who ruled in the name of Charles like a viceroy with power of life and death.

Discontent was spread among troops in Dublin who had not received pay owed to them. When it was considered their morale was sufficiently low Blood and others of the Puritan party in Ireland prepared a plot to seize the person of the Duke of Ormonde and at the same time to capture Dublin Castle. The conspirators believed that in this way they could take over the government of Ireland in a swift but carefully calculated uprising.

The plotters agreed that Blood himself should lead the enterprise, and arrangements were made for the event to occur on March 9th. Blood was again a happy man.

But not for long.

His screening of his fellow conspirators was not thorough. Had it been he would not have included a man named Arden among those at his secret council table. A week before the 9th Arden had a change of heart and betrayed the conspiracy to Ormonde. Blood was lucky. He escaped the snare Ormonde prepared to trap him. His brother-in-law was not so lucky. When Blood heard that his relative had been caught he planned a hasty rescue. It only just failed. But he was then on the run. In Ireland at that time there were not many places he could run to, for he was remembered from the days when he had led Cromwellian troops against the Irish.

He realized there would be no safety for him if he remained, so he left the country of his former triumphs and in due course arrived in Holland. Even so, he was clear away before the story of the part he had played in the conspiracy reached London.

It was not until June 1st, nearly three months after Arden's betrayal, that Samuel Pepys arrived in Whitehall to find the courtiers with only one topic of excited conversation. Blood's plot and the way Ormonde had rounded up all the leaders and then executed them—save one, the ringleader, who had vanished.

But Thomas Blood was not a man who found happiness abroad, where he fancied he was mistrusted. After a brief and very uncomfortable stay in the Low Countries he made his way back to England secretly and returned to London.

There he lived a strange kind of undercover existence, short of funds and almost scared to show his face where it might be recognized. He turned for companionship to that curious and wildly enthusiastic sect who were termed the Fifth Monarchy Men. They were extreme Puritans whose sect had been founded in 1645 to proclaim that the millennium was at hand, when Jesus Christ would return for his second coming and establish on earth the Fifth Universal Monarchy. After eight years of heated emotion they had been broken up by Cromwell himself.

Two years before Thomas Blood made contact with them they had suffered a major setback after the sect had been revived, and nearly a score of them had been arrested, tried, and executed as a menace to the State.

Meeting with such extremists was to attempt swimming in dangerous waters. But the rebel in Blood determined the way he was directed. Another conspiracy produced yet another plot that was badly timed and so failed.

But Blood escaped yet again, only to find himself once more a marked man sought by the authorities. Had he been caught he might have found his neck in danger. But he avoided his hunters it seemed quite safely. So much so that a strange suspicion concerning him grew and became current in the fashionable circles of London.

It was said his hunters did not wish to capture him because he was too useful to the Government. A few who claimed to share momentous matters of State whispered that, while in Holland, the wanted man had made a deal with Whitehall. He had offered his known reputation as a rebel as a cloak that would enable him to circulate among would-be traitors and to win their confidence. He would then pass on to Whitehall what he had learned.

There is no definite evidence that this rumour had any basis in truth, but on the theory that there is no smoke without fire it is at least possible, and nothing known about

Blood at this time suggests otherwise. It is the first piece of mystery surrounding him. Moreover, what is certain is that he wanted nothing so much as the restoration of the Irish lands he had lost and the income he sadly missed.

What can be pointed to is a series of coincidences that are very mysterious in their total suggestion. Just as Blood contacted the Fifth Monarchy Men, urged them to put forward their conspiracy, and then escaped when the plotters were rounded up, so he wriggled out of one tight corner after another, all of a similiar nature, leaving others to answer for the secret intentions they had so ill-advisedly shared with him.

It was surprising how many cells of conspiracy were invaded and destroyed in the 1660's, while Charles did his best to forget the lean times and to indulge himself as a Stuart king with plenty owing to him for what he had suffered in the past.

It is certain that Blood's name was not unfamiliar to the royal ears, but it is doubtful whether during this period there was a meeting between the king on his throne and the man who had served well his royal father's executioners.

Blood made his way by a roundabout route to Scotland, where he made himself known to the restive Covenanters. He was at their council meetings and agreed to fight beside them when they raised the standard of revolt. The rebels made their bid for destiny in a battle fought in the Pentland hills on November 27th, 1666. The rebels suffered an inglorious defeat because the forces of the Crown seemed singularly aware of their strength and the disposition of the Covenanter troops.

But as usual, Thomas Blood escaped the slaughter and actually rode ahead of pursuers back into England, surely the last direction in which to flee if a genuine rebel desired to reach safety.

He was long enough in England to be able to tell

attentive ears what he knew and to accept fresh orders. Then he was travelling westward to Ireland again, seemingly a fugitive. He was not there long, but again perhaps long enough to learn what a man of his reputation could be told in confidence, and then he was heading back across the St. George's Channel to England.

But now the mystery becomes really cloudy. Unless one accepts that Blood wanted to be allowed to perform an act that would again establish him in favour with rebellious elements and win fresh confidence from persons who might be growing suspicious of the curious quality of luck attending his ventures and conspiracies.

Whatever the truth about the Mason rescue, the facts remain to be interpreted as one will. Captain Mason was a rebel and a former friend of Thomas Blood's. He had been taken prisoner in an ill-starred venture and was held in London until the decision was made to send him North to stand trial at the next assizes. Charles's brother the Duke of York is said to have picked personally the eight soldiers who were to escort the prisoner to his trial. Mason's removal occurred at the time of Blood's return to England.

The military escort and their prisoner were approaching Doncaster when four assailants broke from ambush. There was a short sharp engagement, at the end of which the prisoner vanished with the men who had snatched him from his guard, several of whom had been slain.

The attackers were Thomas Blood and three daredevil friends.

When the news of the rescue reached London a price of five hundred pounds was placed on Blood's head. By this time he had vanished again, but with an enhanced reputation as a violent and daring rebel. However, Blood had not left England. He had done his vanishing in Kent, where he posed as a physician named Thomas Allen. In this disguise he remained apparently undiscovered and unmolested while free to meet with other desperate men who plotted ways of ending the Stuart dynasty. If Blood was indeed a spy, and was even being used to lead the rebels into traps during this period of several years, he was neither challenged nor betrayed.

However, by the winter of 1670 the mystery of Colonel Blood was ready to develop in a most interesting fashion. November was a month of State banquets and Court celebrations to mark the occasion of a visit to England by the Prince of Orange. Two dukes attending the revels were bitter enemies. They were those of Buckingham and of Ormonde. The latter was the man who in Ireland had stripped Thomas Blood of the property and pension which had been given to him by Henry Cromwell.

One day when Ormonde left St. James's Palace his coach was held up in St. James's Street by Blood and five other men, who removed the duke from his coach, bound his arms, and hoisted him behind one of the kidnappers. Blood and his companions then spurred for Tyburn, where it was later claimed, their intention was to hang Ormonde on the public gallows. Blood outstripped the others and went ahead, as he told them, to get the gallows ready. Accordingly his curious luck still held when Ormonde decided to put up a fight.

The party were passing Devonshire House at the time when Ormonde forced the rider in front of him to fall from the saddle. But the Duke had to fall with him, for he had been tied to the other man. On the ground the two men rolled, kicking and struggling, while the other four horsemen stood hesitantly watching the pair. The sudden arrival of the duke's coachman sent the mounted men scurrying away. The duke was rescued. Blood was hunted but not found: the colonel was running true to form.

Not surprisingly fresh rumours about him sprang up as soon as news of the escapade reached the Court. It was said the Duke of Buckingham had become Blood's secret patron. Another rumour discounted this one. According to contemporary gossips Blood had not intended to hang Ormonde, but merely to scare him, then hold him prisoner until he agreed to return to his captor the estates he had taken from him.

Whatever the truth, the fact remains that no one was arrested for this bold and unlawful act committed within a short distance of the Court. Thomas Blood seemed to be a man who could flaunt the law of the land safely and not be asked to account for his crimes.

It was not long afterwards that he plotted to hold the King himself to ransom by stealing the Crown jewels, or so it is generally supposed. Others have not been so sure. They have wondered whether Blood might have been encouraged by Charles, who at the time was desperately short of cash. The mystery is another that has never been resolved with certainty.

Certainly Charles had been left little after the Roundheads had grabbed all they could, though even they had not been able to cash the Crown jewels, although Cromwell had held on to them during his lifetime. The Restoration left Charles short of funds and unable to satisfy his favourites, and money for the Crown jewels would have provided badly needed cash if they were stolen.

Thomas Blood prepared a scheme of a kind that was to make him notorious in history. The Crown jewels were kept in the Tower, in the custody of its keeper, an elderly royalist named Talbot Edwards. Such regal and costly ornaments as the Crown, the Sceptre and the Orb were kept in a locked strong-room in the Edwards private apartments. Any thief with enough nerve to attempt to steal the Crown jewels had to get through a closed gateway and then pass an armed guard, before breaking into the strong-room.

Having done that, the thief had to make his getaway after an alarm had been raised.

But Blood had all the nerve the escapade required. Of that there can be no doubt. Of course, if he had Charles's secret backing, that was what a gambler might term his ace in the hole. But of one other thing we can be sure. If Charles was party to the theft there was a clear understanding that the king was not to be involved if the plot miscarried.

Talbot Edwards was a man who took great pride in his office and his charge. He would show the Crown jewels to privileged persons, such as the clergyman and his wife who said that they were about to return to their home in the country after a visit to relatives in London and wished to see the Crown jewels before they left the capital.

They seemed a pleasant pair and Edwards was pleased to oblige them. He had no way of telling that the charming clergyman was Blood himself. The lady remains unknown to this day. She was certainly not the adventurer's wife, for that poor woman was at that time in 1671 lying on a bed of sickness and being cared for by her parents hundreds of miles away in Lancashire.

However, while the phony pair were admiring the displayed gems the woman appeared to be taken ill. She was led to Mrs. Edwards's bed and allowed to lie down after being given some medicine. The man dressed as a clergyman remained with Edwards, discussing the Crown jewels, in the strong-room. When the woman had recovered she left the Tower, leaning heavily on her husband's arm.

A few days later the clergyman returned to the Tower with a gift for Mrs. Edwards. This was a pair of white gloves, in appreciation of her kindness on the day his wife was taken ill so suddenly. The gift was appreciated, and the visitor was in due course introduced to Miss Edwards, a young woman with considerable good looks. Somehow marriage was a subject mentioned naturally, it seemed, by a clergyman who had a nephew recently come of age and who had taken possession of a considerable fortune. He suggested that the nephew should meet Miss Edwards.

Talbot Edwards and his wife were delighted at the idea, and even Miss Edwards seemed interested. The clergyman was pressed to stay to dinner by the entire Edwards family, over which it was arranged for the nephew to pay a call on May 9th. The hour chosen was rather early by today's standards, but three hundred years ago the average person was up soon after day-break, especially in summer. The nephew could be expected at seven in the morning.

When the day for the visit dawned the Edwards family was up and waiting by seven o'clock, when the clergyman and two friends arrived. One of Blood's companions that morning is known to have been a man named Parrot, something of an adventurer, who was later to be hanged for joining the ill-fated rebellion by the Duke of Monmouth. To the somewhat surprised Talbot Edwards the smooth-talking and charming clergyman explained that his nephew was unable to accompany them, but would join them after a short time. While they awaited him, perhaps Mr. Edwards would be kind enough to show the Crown jewels to the clergyman's two friends? Talbot Edwards might not have been so willing to oblige if he had known that a fourth man who certainly wasn't a nephew, remained on guard outside the gateway.

He took his callers into the strong-room, where he was immediately seized and gagged and when he struggled beaten unconscious with mallets concealed inside the visitors' cloaks. When he came to, Blood ran the poor man through with his sword.

The Crown was taken by Blood himself, crushed in his hands, and held flat under his cloak. The Orb disappeared in a most unlikely place—inside Parrot's baggy breeches.

The Crown was taken by Blood himself . . .

A file was produced and the task of cutting the Sceptre in half was begun, but was not completed before the fourth man, the one on guard, raised the alarm. He had been seen by Miss Edwards' maid, who had been on the lookout for the nephew. Maid and mistress both supposed the man to be the expected nephew, and waited for him to announce his arrival.

They were still waiting when the girl's brother, young Talbot Edwards, arrived home on leave from Flanders, where his regiment was stationed. He was stopped by the lookout, but broke away and went to seek his parents. He was explaining to his mother what had occurred outside when the father's voice was heard calling, 'The Crown is stolen! Treason!' The son ran to the open strong-room, found his father bathed in blood, the damaged Sceptre thrown on the floor, and the Crown and Orb missing—like Blood and his companions, who had left without raising the suspicions of the regular guard. However, they were still on Tower Hill when the young man on leave from Flanders found the captain of the Tower Guard and raised the alarm.

Parrot had no wish to be caught with the Orb in his breeches. He threw it away and took to his heels. Blood's other companion, unhampered by the abandoned Sceptre, also got away. Blood was not so fortunate. For once his luck was out. He had reached his horse and mounted, only for the animal to slip on the cobbles and pitch its rider headlong. Before Blood could take to flight on foot he was captured.

He and the Crown returned to the Tower.

Within a short while the whole of London was agog at the news of what had happened that bright May morn. But while the citizens waited for news of Blood being brought to trial, and waited in vain, the captured adventurer was desperately trying to make terms with his captors. It was known that he had been interrogated by Dr. Chamberlain, who had called on Sir William Waller to support him, but to both men Blood gave the same obstinate reply.

'I will talk to no one but the king himself.'

It was a bold and even desperate line to take, for Blood was a man with a price on his head already. Amazingly, Charles, when told agreed to interview the prisoner.

Charles's giving in to what was very nearly a demand by the prisoner gave plenty of food for speculation as to why. Did the king wish to make sure that Blood would keep faith about a deal that had been made in secret? Was Blood gambling on that being the case and wanting fresh proof that Charles would ensure there was no prosecution?

Those two questions are part of the fabric of mystery still surrounding the character of Colonel Thomas Blood three hundred years later.

Whatever the rightful answers, Blood was taken to an interview with the man whose crown he had stolen. Before Charles the prisoner put on a spirited display, telling the one-time royal fugitive that the English Crown was something any man might risk his life for, a comment that brought a smile of appreciation to the royal lips, for Charles certainly found himself admiring a villain who could be charming. Charles asked about the Ormonde kidnapping, and Blood replied at once that he was the organizer and had done so for revenge because he had suffered at the duke's hands.

What was said to have won Charles's admiration for the man who had put his head in peril was Blood's statement that not long before he had gone to Battersea to assassinate the monarch while the latter was bathing, but had been restrained by sight of a man who filled him with awe.

'For that reason I was unable to do Your Majesty ill,' Blood said firmly. 'I was captivated.'

The entire claim could have been a lie, but if so it was

both calculated and clever. Charles admired the boldness of a man who could speak up in this way. Moreover, he did not find the sentiment expressed at all distasteful. The dialoguc between the Crown's legal wearer and the man who had stolen it continued. When the two men who seemed to have a correct evalution of each other parted Thomas Blood had been pardoned for all his crimes including those he was said to have committed. The bold line he had taken had indeed paid handsome dividends.

Even more surprising, Blood was very soon again in possession of the estates taken from him by the Duke of Ormonde.

Who was responsible for this enormous and almost incredible change in the adventurer's fortunes? Had there indeed been a secret understanding between the thief and the owner of the Crown whereby Charles, always pressed for cash, might reline an empty purse? Or had there been a secret understanding with the Duke of Buckingham, now suddenly the admitted patron of Colonel Blood, the former Roundhead? Certainly Buckingham introduced the man who had talked boldly to Charles to Court circles, and within a short while, from being a hunted fugitive, Thomas Blood was a fashionable guest at the homes of Ministers of the Crown. It was in such a home that John Evelyn the diarist met the man of forceful and determined charm. Evelyn remained unimpressed.

He went home and penned in his diary: 'This man had not only a daring but a villainous, unmerciful look, a false countenance, but very well spoken and dangerously insinuating.'

The diarist was one of the growing number of people in London at the time who came to believe that this man who lived such a charmed life, in most meanings of the term, did so for only one reason—he was a secret agent for Charles and Buckingham. But there is no proof. The secret surrounding Colonel Blood is one that no researcher has solved. This could mean that where his interests lay Blood was a man who kept faith—at a price. That price would include freedom from arrest and trial.

All England waited to learn that the man who had planned and executed a daring plot to steal the Crown jewels and had been captured because his horse stumbled was being brought to trial.

Blood continued his new life as a favourite among Court circles and was not brought to trial. The Crown jewels had been restored to the Tower. The Edwards family had smoothed their ruffled feathers and did their best to ignore the comments of false friends. The plot and its failure ceased to be a nine days' wonder or even one of nine weeks. After all, now he had seemingly no need to hide his face. Blood showed it daily in the most fashionable taverns and meeting-places of the town.

Yet with the passage of time a change came over his choice of tavern for regular drinking. He left the notable Royalist haunts and was seen daily seated with a tankard on a settle seat of an inn near Westminster market, where a number of men who had been Roundhead officers met together.

Was Thomas Blood back at his suspected secret trade of spy? Again there is no real answer to the mystery of the man. He maintained to any who were interested enough to inquire that he was by religion a Presbyterian, a Noncomformist sect at that time not only out of favour but considered with a good deal of suspicion by Ministers whose task included the security of the realm.

Because Blood did not try to hide the nature of his religious convictions—if indeed that is what they were—he again became suspect to men like Ormonde, who had never trusted him. When in 1679 a Presbyterian plot to further revolt was reported and a man named Dangerfield confessed to being involved he named Thomas Blood as a man who would lead a section of the rising.

Colonel Blood, Dangerfield maintained, would be made a major-general if the plot was successful. But the plot was never put to the proof and again Blood's involvement is something that can only be debated, not decided one way or the other. However, perhaps it is not without point that in the following year, 1680, he was arrested on the order of the Duke of Buckingham, who had been his powerful patron. He had recently quarrelled with Buckingham, something he should have avoided doing if he had been well advised.

Again there was rumour of a plot. Blood was said to have been scheming to bring a list of charges against the duke, including a number of serious crimes. The most one can say is that Blood, who should have known better from his own experiences, once spoke unwisely about Buckingham when sharp and unfriendly ears were listening. Not long afterwards Buckingham took proceedings against the man to whom he had shown high favour a few years before and claimed damages of ten thousand pounds.

Evading an armed enemy was one thing. Avoiding officers of a court of law was very different. If Blood ran this time there was no way to creep back under protection. He stayed, was arrested, and in some way found enough cash to have himself released on bail.

Again London waited to see the spectacle of the amazing adventurer placed on trial. Once more the citizens of the capital waited in vain, and were keenly disappointed.

Before he could be brought to trial Blood became ill. Within a short while he was dead. The date was August 24th, 1680. He was buried only for fresh rumours to arise. These maintained that the burial had been a sham, that Blood had not died, but escaped. The local coroner felt it necessary to do something to stop them. He ordered an inquest to be held. For this purpose the grave was reopened and the body exhumed and produced for formal identifying.

It was placed on the record that the body was that of Thomas Blood and that the dead man had died of natural causes. A great many rumours were buried with the body that was returned to its grave.

Not that gossiping tongues were short of a subject. A non-violent death for the mysterious adventurer who had cheated the hangman, as many believed, seemed truly an anti-climax. Most things Thomas Blood had done in his lifetime had given rise to rumours and gossip, and in this regard he had not been inconsistent in his dying.

But what of the secrets he carried with him to the grave?

Today we can only speculate. Was he a spy whose secret worth guaranteed his freedom from prosecution and trial? Did he betray plotting rebels? Had he a secret understanding with the king himself and was this why Buckingham dared to become his sponsor at Court?

If there are no sure and certain answers to such questions, at least Thomas Blood sounded a warning that has not gone unheeded in the past three hundred years. No other bold adventurer has been given a chance of stealing the Crown jewels. In more than one way Colonel Thomas Blood taught his contemporaries quite a few harsh lessons on the subject of State security.

7

The Disappearance of Amelia Earhart

Soon after Colonel Lindbergh had made his historic flight solo across the Atlantic to Paris an American publisher had the idea to seek a woman aviator and back her to imitate Lindbergh's example and become the first woman to span the Atlantic in an aircraft.

Apart from her making history, she would have a story to tell which George Palmer Putnam believed would make a best-selling book for his firm. However, any woman who took up the challenge of being groomed for such a flight in the year 1928 had to be an exceptional person. For one thing she had to be a dedicated flier, and in that year not too many dedicated women fliers were to be found, though Italy, France, Britain, and America were to produce a surprising number in the years ahead.

However, looking back nearly half a century from today, it is easy to believe that much of the inspiration towards flying discovered by women who became famous fliers in the thirties stemmed from the example of the young woman finally chosen by G. P. Putnam. On that day he received a visitor in his office, and saw a smiling young woman with crisp curly hair and a pair of wide bright eyes coming towards him with an air of confidence that registered instantly with him.

Before a word was spoken between the woman who had arrived to be interviewed and the publisher who was to interview her the man seated behind his desk had a hunch he had found the female flier he sought. He wanted someone keen but who was essentially a woman and not a female acting like a man. He wished her to be modest yet having assurance and courage, for whoever was chosen would have to face the possibility of meeting death suddenly. Moreover, he wanted a female who knew when to keep her own counsel. He didn't require a chatterer, however bright her chatter might be.

The publisher rose and shook hands with his smiling visitor. He noted with approval that she had a firm handclasp.

'My name's Amelia Earhart,' she told him. 'I'm a social worker.'

The interview went smoothly. The visitor explained that she was thirty and the daughter of a lawyer in Kansas. She had lived an outdoor life in her early years and had become interested in aircraft and flying in the last year of the First World War, when she had served as a nursing aide in a Canadian military hospital in Toronto.

Since the end of the war she had spent some time in medical school, but she had also worked as a car mechanic and a commercial photographer.

The man behind the desk received the impression that this confident young woman was a person of parts.

'How and when did you first become interested in flying? I know it's your hobby, but how did it come to have a personal appeal to you, Miss Earhart?' he inquired.

She told him how she had gone with her father to an air meeting in California in 1920 and had watched spellbound as the pilots performed what were then called 'stunts' in their flimsy biplanes that had looked to the young Amelia Earhart to be miracles of canvas and cane that were pulled all over the sky by a spluttering engine that sent a two-bladed propeller whirring at a speed that raised a cloud of dust from the dry soil of the airfield.

Before she left that first air display she had taken a 'joy ride' in one of those planes. For her it really was a ride of joy. She thrilled to the small plane's motion and watched in genuine fascination how the pilot turned his fragile aircraft to right and to left, making it climb or plunge earthwards at will.

From that moment mere casual interest that had been aroused in Canada talking to wounded airmen was changed to a strong desire to be able to fly, to be one of those beings who could imitate the birds of the air and enjoy a freedom unknown to the mere earthbound.

'That was when I realized I had to become a flier,' she told Putnam. 'While I was enjoying that joy ride in California. After the plane had landed I told my father. He laughed.'

But Edwin Earhart soon came to realize that his earnest young daughter had not been joking with him after she had enrolled for flying tuition. Three years later she shepherded her aircraft alone under the critical gaze of an examiner for the Fédération Aéronautique. She brought it to a smooth landing, and when she saw the examiner smiling she knew she had earned the prize she most desired, the Fédération's international pilot's licence. That piece of paper allowed her to fly where she wished. It was her passport to the open sky.

For three years she tried to make a livelihood out of her ability to fly an aircraft. She failed. Women fliers were human novelties. The jobs went to their masculine competitors. After three years of trying in vain to break into a man's world she accepted defeat and in 1926 became a social worker in Boston. However, the desire to fly whenever she could remained in her.

She envied the four women who had tried to follow in Lindbergh's flying steps only to fail.

Putnam told her of a fifth woman who had wanted to fly

but was being prevented by members of her family. She was a woman who owned an aircraft and her name was Mrs. Guest.

'She wants a suitable woman to take her place, Miss Earhart, and I'd like to know if you would be willing.'

Amelia Earhart's eyes opened to their widest.

Before she could speak the watchful man opposite, who had agreed to find a suitable substitute for Mrs. Guest, went on.

'I know of your flying activities, Miss Earhart,' he told his visitor. 'For instance, I'm aware that you were the first female aviator to reach an altitude of fourteen thousand feet and I've been informed that you've experimented with air-cooled engines. So I'm reasonably sure that you are the kind of person Mrs. Guest is looking for to join the crew of her *Friendship*, which is to make a transatlantic flight shortly.'

When she left that office Amelia Earhart was a woman stepping out of a dream, and she knew she could do that with every confidence, for the dream had come true. She was to fly with a well-known pilot named Wilmer Stultz on another bid to cross the Atlantic by air.

It was on the 17th June, 1928, that *Friendship*, with Stultz at the controls, lifted from the harbour at Trepassey, in Newfoundland, and almost at once flew into a belt of descending fog as her nose turned eastwards.

Another death-challenging flight had begun.

Friendship was a three-engined Fokker which had been fitted with floats, and besides the pilot and mechanic Louis Gordon, who was usually called Slim, Amelia Earhart was the only other person aboard. Even so, the aircraft was almost dangerously overloaded for such a flight, as Stultz discovered to his dismay when he ran into a series of violent air storms that left him flying blind with controls that informed him his aircraft was becoming sluggish and unresponsive. It was a flight during which the pilot had to take chances, for ice formed and he had to drop almost to wave height to get rid of it. Then he had to get that unresponsive aircraft away from those threatening white crests of water.

Suddenly an engine coughed. The coughing was taken up by the second engine, and then the third. Gordon became a worried man. He turned to the radio, only to find the set was dead. He began to use up fuel fast to keep those engines from coughing.

Friendship's flight became a race against time and the elements. The only woman member of the crew occupied herself with writing her impressions in the logbook she had brought. Some of those impressions were graphic, as when she wrote, 'Clouds like fantastic gobs of mashed potatoes.'

Those words might never have been read by millions of readers had Gordon not kept those engines pulling and if Stultz had lost his battle with the headwinds he was meeting. But the fuel lasted and Stultz kept his aircraft flying until he reached Wales and came down on his floats in Burry Port after living through the most danger-fraught twenty hours of his life.

When Amelia Earhart climbed out of the eleventh aircraft to cross the Atlantic she had for personal luggage besides her well-filled logbook a toothbrush and a comb.

When the news was flashed to the United States that *Friendship* and her crew of three had landed safely in the British Isles the most relieved person in North America was the man who had accepted Amelia Earhart for the flight, George Palmer Putnam.

When she returned to America he asked her to become his wife.

'Marriage will not interfere with your flying,' he assured her.

They were duly married and Amelia Earhart was suddenly a woman with two lives to live. One was the life of a famous flier who was seldom out of the public's gaze, the other that private life in which she found a haven to retire to as Mrs. G. P. Putnam when the pressures of publicity and press campaigns became overwhelming.

Everytime she took to the air reporters and cameramen were on hand, for she became not only a breaker of flying records, but a pioneer in her own right. She flew autogyros when those fore-runners of the modern helicopter were little more than in the experimental stage. She tested new engines and aircraft. She wrote articles for the Press on aviation and appeared on forums where flying was debated. Her book with the quotations from her log of the *Friendship* flight became a best-seller under the Putnam imprint. She found time for literary lunches and talks.

Not surprisingly she made friends everywhere. There was a warmth to her nature that made strangers respond openly to her. If she had a secret dream during the four years after stepping ashore in Wales it was to fly an aircraft solo across the Atlantic.

When her flying log had a recorded thousand hours she decided she must prepare for what she considered the big test. She began intensive instruction in blind flying with only instruments to guide her. She studied stellar navigation. She also made ready a single-engined Lockheed-Vega craft which was painted a vivid red.

In the early summer 1932 she was ready. On the 20th of May, with the sun westering, she lifted the Lockheed-Vega into the air at Harbour Grace, in Newfoundland, waved to the crowd below, and then settled down in the cockpit and pushed a few stray curls under the brim of her flying helmet.

She was alone, flying in the wake of Lindbergh and *Friendship* over a waste of waters that remained unbroken for almost fifteen hours. When at length she saw land it was the Irish coast.

Amelia Earhart lifted the Lockheed-Vega into the air . . .

Tired but feeling happy and thrilled by her achievement, she followed the example of the first fliers to cross the Atlantic from the New World to the Old, Alcock and Brown, who had landed in an Irish bog thirteen years before. She nosed the red Lockheed-Vega down to a safe landing in a field not far from Londonderry. The only observers waiting in the field were some cattle that ran bellowing before she cut the engine.

The tired woman who climbed from the red plane to stand stretching her aching limbs in the lush green meadow of the Emerald Isle had made the crossing in fourteen hours and fifty-six minutes, thereby establishing another flying record.

It was one, however, attended by great hazard for most of the passage. When the true story of that flight was told aviators all over the world marvelled at this woman's courage and will to win. Four hours away from Harbour Grace there had been an acrid smell of burning in the cockpit as tongues of flame licked through a cracked manifold ring, which could have melted or split apart had she not been a superlative flier able to keep the Lockheed-Vega on an even keel, even when she ran into a fierce and prolonged Atlantic thunderstorm, during which lightning played around the red plane like St. Elmo's fire.

She had no thought of turning back. She flew on to another crisis when her altimeter ceased to function. From that moment she was flying, in the earlier naval phrase, by guess and by God. She was forced to climb. Ice glazed the red wings. The additional weight turned the little aircraft's nose down. That was a collection of bad moments during which Amelia Earhart fought the controls of a malfunctioning engine to level off a plane that seemed suddenly to have grown a will of its own.

For a third of her time over the Atlantic she was flying blind through storms. The instrument that told her how many revolutions per minute the single engine was making stopped providing that important information when its needle fell back and did not lift again. Wind pressures and storm turbulence brought on a leak in the lead to the fuel gauge. The cockpit filled with petrol fumes.

In the circumstances she was not surprisingly glad to sight land. Any thought of continuing farther left her mind. Her luck had held—amazingly. Only a fool would continue such a hazardous flight, and Amelia Earhart was a level-headed woman capable of facing facts and abiding by her own calm judgment of them.

When the full story was told of that incredible record-breaking flight alone over thousands of miles of ocean, by a woman who saw the odds mounting against her hourly, Amelia Earhart was hailed as a heroine. She was the First Woman of the Skies so far as the general public was concerned, both in America and in Europe, the pioneer who had shown what a woman flying solo could achieve. To her own sex she had demonstrated that in flying prowess a woman could equal the achievements of men and even surpass them.

She returned to her own country to continue her career in aviation, working to demonstrate that air travel was something in the shape of things to come. She helped to make the world of her day a smaller place and so promoted movement among peoples which in turn made for greater understanding.

When, three years after the Atlantic solo flight, she made a similar flight of almost the same length, her fresh triumph was accepted by the world's press almost as a matter of course. The world had come to expect extraordinary feats of flying skill and daring from this most unusual woman who was dedicated to her career in aviation and the interests it furthered.

That solo flight of nearly twenty-five hundred miles in

1935 was made from Honolulu to California. She arrived in Oakland to great acclaim, and she stepped from her plane looking fresh and happy. This later flight had been made in a comfortable pilot's cabin, and on the flight she had enjoyed a warm meal.

Conditions in aviation were changing, and Amelia Earhart was doing more than anybody to bring about these changes.

It was after that flight that she came to sense that one day her luck, which had held in amazing fashion, might run out. Flying and taking the risks attending flying in those days had made her both a realist and a fatalist.

She admitted as much when she confessed, 'Some day I'll get bumped off. I don't want to go, but when I go I'd like to go in my plane. Quickly,' she added after a brief pause.

It was almost as though she expected to lose her life flying.

She planned her most ambitious flight. It was to be one that took her around the world. Her circumnavigation of the globe would, in her own opinion, be the peak of her flying career. Such a flight could not be undertaken alone. But she planned to take off with only one companion, an expert navigator. The navigator she chose, who felt honoured to accompany her, was Fred Noonan.

Again the world prepared to follow the flight made by the woman who had been dubbed 'Lady Lindy' by her admirers in the United States.

Once more it was summer. The year 1937. The aircraft she was to fly was a twin-engined Lockheed Electra monoplane. Before it was airborne disaster struck. The plane, weighed down with full tanks of petrol, didn't lift as expected and flopped back on the ground. The damage caused meant an extensive delay, and before the repaired plane was again ready to take off the weather had changed sufficiently to make the pilot and her navigator alter their plans.

Instead of beginning the round-the-world flight by flying westward to Howland Island, which is an ocean speck in the Pacific north of Samoa, they would fly on a reverse itinerary, going east at the start, and making the trip to Howland the last leg of the flight.

The superstitious have since claimed that this changed Amelia Earhart's luck. However, there have been other reasons put forward to explain why the world flight was never completed. Therein lies the mystery of Amelia Earhart.

What is known for certain is that the Lockheed Electra winged its way without misadventure round three-quarters of the world to reach Lae, in New Guinea. By that time the fliers had covered almost twenty-three thousand miles. When they had refuelled to take off from New Guinea they would have to make a long hop of two thousand five hundred miles to Howland before landing again.

It was not a stage of the famous world flight to daunt a pilot who had years before flown solo similar distances from Honolulu to America and from Canada to Europe, but much would depend on the navigational skill of the man working over his charts with squares and dividers. Fred Noonan's job was to plot a course to a Pacific island not much more than two miles across, a coral speck in the ocean that could be missed in low cloud conditions. Moreover, it was not a course that crossed many known shipping lanes.

The Lockheed Electra, with the name *Lady Lindy* written on the fuselage in honour of the pilot flying her, had her tanks replenished at Lae, and on July 1st climbed into the sky over New Guinea and headed on course.

Ahead of Amelia Earhart was six or seven thousand miles of flying to complete the first aerial navigation of the globe. How many of the miles to Howland she flew is not known.

What is known is that *Lady Lindy* flew into violent headwinds, and some hours after taking off from Lae the pilot's voice was heard by a U.S. Coast Guard cutter. In a calm voice Amelia Earhart spoke of the headwinds. There was a good deal of atmospherics making reception of her call indistinct at times.

But she was heard to say the words, 'Half an hour's gas.' There was more crackling over the radio receiver aboard the Coast Guard cutter, and then came clearly the word, 'Circling.'

That could only mean one thing.

Lady Lindy was lost. The incredible had happened. Two of the most experienced fliers in the world had missed their way to that small atoll in the Marshall group of islands.

How could this have happened?

That was the question asked immediately the news was broadcast to the world. It has never been answered satisfactorily although a number of curious and even fantastic answers have been suggested, one as recently as November 1970.

When told of that broken radio message from Amelia Earhart and of *Lady Lindy*'s failure to arrive at Howland, President Roosevelt gave immediate orders that resulted in a dozen craft of the U.S. Navy making a search of a quarter of a million square miles of the Pacific in the hope of finding the lost plane or even trace of it.

Officially the search was abandoned only when all expectation of finding any clue to the mystery was given up. *Lady Lindy* had vanished.

The well-known American columnist, Walter Lippmann, wrote a touching epitaph to America's lost Lady Lindy.

'The world is a better place to live in,' he said, 'because it contains human beings who will give up ease and security and stake their own lives in order to do what they themselves think worth doing. They do the useless, brave, noble, the divinely foolish and the very wisest things that are done by man.'

He went on to state the value of their singleness of mind when he added, 'And what they prove to themselves and to others is that man is no mere creature of his habits, no mere automaton in his routine, but that in the dust of which he is made there is also fire, lighted now and then by great winds from the sky.'

Such a 'great wind' had burned to fullest brightness the genius of the woman who was Amelia Earhart. It may even have been the cause of that fire being put out.

Two years later, in 1939, while the world was still wondering what had gone wrong to cause the world flight to end in disaster and silence, a probate court in the United States accepted the official verdict that had been recorded of 'lost at sea' and granted the estate she had left to the man who had married her and given her the chance to achieve fame.

Within a short while the Second World War had begun, and it was not till it had run its grim six years and hostilities had ceased that the mystery of Amelia Earhart's vanishing became a challenge to a number of persons who studied it. That was when the curious rumours started to circulate. One of them centred about the suggestion that her vanishing was a device to aid the American Government of the time. By becoming officially lost the news had justified that extensive search by units of the U.S. Navy, which had cruised among the Marianas, islands held by the Japanese under a League of Nations mandate. For some time the belief had existed that the Japanese, contrary to the terms of their mandate and to international law, had been fortifying the Marianas as secret naval bases. Why?

The answer to that question was suggested indirectly in a film made in Hollywood in 1943, while the United States and Japan were at war.

ss, why did not Emperor Hirohito tell the truth? The orists claimed to have the answer to this question. It was, hort, that at the time of Japan's surrender the Emperor de a deal with the Americans. This amounted to hand- over his captive and what she knew, 'which could be barrassing to the U.S. Government,' for a promise of not ng tried as a war criminal.

ndependent inquirers who still sought an answer to the stery which already had too many answers, most of them flicting, sought the opinion of Mrs. Albert Morrissey at home in West Medford, Massachusetts. Mrs. Morrissey s Amelia Earhart's sister.

The photographs of Mrs. Bolam,' she said very positively, not even look like my sister. Why should they? My er is dead.'

But the same cannot be said of the mystery remaining er the silence following that broken radio call on the 2nd July, 1937. Indeed, the mystery of Amelia Earhart ows every likelihood of growing and even providing still ther conflicting solutions.

Amelia Earhart and Fred Noonan had been spies for the United States.

But there has been no official agreement or denial. On the other hand it became known some while after the ill-fated flight was history that President Roosevelt had personally authorized the spending of considerable sums to make a sound airstrip for landing on Howland. Moreover, he had given unpublicized orders, as is known today, for American naval craft to be stationed along the line of flight from Lae. As navigational aids for Fred Noonan? Or for some other reason, such as being available for that intensive search throughout two hundred and fifty thousand miles of the Pacific?

So intrigued were a number of researchers into the mystery that several made a particular study of all that was known about the flight and events before and since it was made. They tried to fit their findings into a kind of jigsaw puzzle to obtain a clear picture of what the flight really meant to persons not known to be concerned with it.

The Pacific islands were visited. A great deal of research was undertaken, and as the result of a book that was published on *The Search for Amelia Earhart* members of the American Congress in Washington tabled a motion calling for a Congressional Committee to be established to inquire into all aspects of the disappearance of Amelia Earhart and her navigator.

A theory based on the visits to the Pacific which provided the material for this book suggested that Amelia Earhart's plane actually crashed about five hundred miles off course. The further suggestion was that the pilot was only slightly injured when she and Fred Noonan were made prisoner by the Japanese, who considered they had come as spies.

If that is indeed what happened, then there must have been a valid reason for an expert navigator like Fred

Noonan being that distance off his true course, which was no secret.

However, the mystery becomes more involved, for apparently further patient inquiry revealed other facts which pointed to the prisoners having been taken to the known Japanese military headquarters in the Pacific, Saipan. There, according to this suggestion, the story ended in tragedy. Amelia Earhart went down with a savage attack of dysentery and died. That left only Fred Noonan knowing the real story. To be certain that he did not become a witness against them, so ran the enlarged theory, he was shot by the Japanese officially for spying in a military region.

How much of this claim can be proven it is not easy to discover. But alongside it can be placed another claim resulting from patient research and inquiry. At Saipan was fought one of the hardest engagements of the Pacific war before the fortified base fell to the attacking American forces. Later some American Marines were told to dig up an unmarked grave in one of the native cemeteries. Two bodies were taken from this unidentified grave, and these were flown to the United States. This fact was established after interviews with some of the Marines who had been at Saipan. When the claim was made in the United States there was no reaction from official Washington.

Where were those two bodies taken?

That is another of the unanswered questions. Yet another is, why does Washington continue silent about the truth? Why can't the truth be told after more than thirty years?

There have been a number of suggested answers to this last question. It is argued that, if Washington really knows the secret of what happened to the fliers in *Lady Lindy*, they are reluctant to make it officially known for fear of intimidating the Japanese, who would be reluctant to admit, in any case, that Noonan had been executed and

that Amelia Earhart had not received medi
competent to save her life.

There is one other factor that must be we
the other elements of the mystery. Anyone e
various claims and suggestions would ask, ve
why was no visit made to the Marianas and Sa
truth established within a reasonable time o
World War ending.

The answer to that particular question is rea

After the war that region of the Pacific wa
by the Americans, and the Central Intellig
began training some of its secret agents in an a
out of bounds to anyone wishing to make in
what had happened and what was happening
region is still a secret area where interconti
ballistic missiles are tested.

So the mystery remains, offering a bright c
more theorists with alternative solutions.

The most surprising was offered towards the
when two American Air Force officers claimed
Earhart was alive at the time and living as
Bolam. To support this new claim they said th
covered that *Lady Lindy* had been forced down
ception near Hill Island in the Phoenix Group, c
1937—the day after leaving Lae. The interce
Japanese aircraft from an aircraft carrier. For t
of the Second World War, according to the cla
female captive was held prisoner in Tokio—i
peror's Imperial Palace.

Mrs. Bolam was sought, but she denied bei
Earhart. She also displayed a marked dislike for
questions about her past. This was not surprisin
an elderly lady of seventy-two—which would
Amelia Earhart's age had she lived.

If this theory was based on anything other th

8

The Lonely Man on Devil's Isle

Possibly the most famous, and at the same time, infamous, prison settlement in the history of the world was Devil's Island, which is a large rock rising from the seabed about ten miles off the mainland of French Guiana, in South America. On a foggy day anyone looking for it could miss it, for it is only a little over thirty acres in size. But a foggy day in that tropical region is a rare event. The prisoners of the past would have welcomed fog to relieve the uncomfortable wearisomeness of heat and flies and sickness due to poor food, harsh conditions, and the knowledge that one had been sent there to die, forgotten.

However, one man who was sent to Devil's Isle early in 1895, branded a traitor to his country, was not forgotten. He not only survived the ordeal of prison life on the island, but lived to return to France and be vindicated, have his name cleared, and to die honoured, hailed as a hero and martyr.

But while he spent nearly five terrible years on Devil's Isle he was more lonely than he had ever been in his life. He could not know that his cause was being championed in France while he suffered in a steamy jungle heat thousands of miles on the other side of the world.

For those years Alfred Dreyfus was probably the most lonely man on Devil's Isle.

He had been a captain in the French Army who had one day walked into a mystery. Much of that mystery still remains. It began, for Alfred Dreyfus, on October 15th,

1894, which was a bright autumn day in Paris. That morning he left his home dressed as a civilian and set out on foot to reach a building in the Rue Saint-Dominique. It was an undistinguished building save for the guard outside, whose presence proclaimed that it housed the French Ministry of War.

Alfred Dreyfus had been summoned to an interview.

As he walked through the Paris streets his mind was uneasy because the interview, when he had been notified of it, had been formally described as a general inspection. To Dreyfus this had only one meaning. He was being summoned to be severely criticized or censured, and he had no idea what he had done to earn such an unwelcome summons to the Ministry.

Very possibly as he walked in the autumn sunshine he felt anxious about the outcome, for no officer relished one of these politely termed general inspections, which usually could be described more accurately as a general dressing-down. But very certainly there was no thought in his mind that morning of the notorious penal settlement off the coast of French Guiana reserved for enemies of the State, where at night each prisoner was fettered and locked up for twelve hours, from six in the evening until six the next morning.

Still less that he would, within a matter of months, be voyaging there in the black-hulled convict ship *Martinier*, a man disgraced and ruined, notorious as a traitor denounced by his superiors.

However, he was not left long in doubt that something was seriously amiss with his military career after he walked into the building in the Rue Saint-Dominique. He gave his name and explained that he had an appointment, and was shown into a room where he was confronted by three men, all of whom looked not only grave but threatening in the manner in which they received him.

One of them was from the bureau Dreyfus knew to be responsible for military training and general operations. His name was Major Mercier du Paty de Clam. There was only enmity in his bright eyes that morning.

Another was a police commissaire named Cochefort, so there was the suggestion that the general inspection concerned a possibly criminal matter, and not surprisingly Dreyfus became worried.

The third man to confront him was the archivist responsible for the Ministry's records, a Monsieur Gribelin.

Sitting apart from these principals was a man with a notebook and writing material. This was the police commissaire's secretary.

There was one odd note in that office. Major Paty de Clam had a large bandage wrapped around the thumb of his right hand. It was a very fresh bandage, as Dreyfus could see.

What he was unable to see, of course, was that the bandaged thumb was in no way injured or damaged. The bandage was a device towards an end. It was to give the major a seeming excuse not to write something he preferred to have Dreyfus write at his dictation.

The so-called inspection began. The known life and career of Captain Alfred Dreyfus was hurriedly gone over for the record.

The man in civilian clothes facing the three-man tribunal listened to the potted story of his life like someone in a daze, unable to believe that this was happening to him—or even why.

He heard himself give verbal replies in a low voice he scarcely recognized as his own. He was a captain of the General Staff, he agreed, although that appointment had a qualification attached. He was what was officially designated a *stagiaire*. In effect, this description meant that he was a General Staff captain on probation, who had need of proving himself before the appointment was made permanent.

That appointment had been made on the first day of the previous year.

He told the tribunal that he was born in Alsace, in the industrial town of Mulhouse, where his family owned a number of prosperous textile mills.

'I am thirty-five,' he said. 'I celebrated my thirty-fifth birthday only a few days ago.'

'You are a Jew?' he was asked.

'I am,' he said.

He knew very well that this fact had in the past served to segregate him from his brother officers. At that time there was a marked anti-semitic feeling in France, particularly in the Services. On the French General Staff there were high-ranking officers who felt they had cause to distrust Jews for being too internationally minded. This was the reason usually given for any expressed doubt about the quality of a Jewish officer's patriotism.

When Dreyfus saw the reaction to his statement he knew he was in some measure in that room and answering the questions of these three men because of his race.

He had understood very well the extreme disadvantage his race and faith had provided in his military career. The prospect had not stopped him because he wanted to serve his country as a serving officer. He had joined the artillery. After all, he had been set a good example. By no less a man than Napoleon himself.

The details of his marriage were gone over. He had married Lucie Hadamard in 1889, and he had two children. The boy was Pierre, the girl Jeanne.

Next his career and his service until he had been gazetted a captain in the Fourteenth Regiment of Artillery. He admitted not living on his captain's pay. He was in receipt of a regular income from his shares in the family's Mulhouse textile mills.

This placing of everything about him on record in that office, and the probing that accompanied his answers to questions, became more threatening as time wore away. The police commissaire's secretary was busily scribbling, the Ministry archivist was shuffling his sheaf of multi-coloured papers, while the major nursed that ridiculously bandaged thumb and continued to read out the questions he had prepared before Alfred Dreyfus's arrival.

The questioning came to the time when Dreyfus had been interviewed by General Bonnefort, chief of the Military Selection Committee. This was in answer to his application for entrace to the Ecole Supérieure de Guerre, or General Staff College. Dreyfus had been made aware of the general's anti-semitic feelings as soon as he entered the interviewing-room. He didn't have to be told that the report on him would be unfavourable.

Just how unfavourable his placing revealed. On the list of applications returned to General Bonnefort the name of Alfred Dreyfus was in third place among the recommendations. When that list left the general's hands it had dropped to ninth. As it chanced, General Bonnefort's opinion was not upheld by other members of the Military Selection Committee, but when Dreyfus was accepted as a probationary Staff officer there was one firm mark of disapproval against the selection. This open disagreement with the majority's decision was signed by General Bonnefort.

However, while the probing and formalities continued Dreyfus became more and more aware that something was known to his questioners that they were not prepared to share with him—at least, not at this stage of the proceedings. This awareness made him feel not only uneasy, but unable to keep from being fearful of the outcome of this long session.

And always his uneasy gaze returned to the bandaged thumb. Somehow it seemed to menace him as the major waggled it to and fro over the papers on his desk.

Dreyfus knew that his fate might be decided by what those papers contained. This certainty only added to his unease, which became visible to the men watching him, as though expecting him to betray some sign of guilt.

But about what?

As a matter of fact, the papers lying under the hand with the bandaged thumb contained details of a secret report that had caused no small flutter in the French War Ministry. They were secret because they concerned something that had happened three months before, in the summer of that year of 1894, and only now was anything being done because a snooper had threatened a man who was covering up for a friend, and a scapegoat had to be found.

Alfred Dreyfus certainly had the feeling that his interview was directed towards making him some kind of scapegoat, but he had no suspicion about the reason.

Three months before an anonymous letter had been sent to the German Military Attaché in Paris. This was Colonel Max von Schwartzkoppen, who was at the time a very popular figure in Paris, one who spent money freely in entertaining his very many friends. The anonymous letter was left in the military attaché's office. When he looked for it later it had disappeared. The letter arrived in the office of a French major. This officer was attached to what was termed the Statistical Section of the War Ministry.

His name was Herbert Joseph Henry. He was a man advancing in years who had risen from the ranks after seeing considerable action in Africa with one of the native Zouave regiments. He had no General Staff training and had not gone through the regular college channels, but he had been selected for a position in the Deuxième Bureau because he had been warmly recommended by General de

Boisdeffre, the Chief of the General Staff, who had a high regard for Henry's qualities as a serving soldier and as an officer capable of sound Intelligence work. The Deuxième Bureau was the department that dealt with counter-espionage.

As to the letter that had mysteriously found itself into Henry's hands, it was to become famous as the cause of Alfred Dreyfus's ruin and virtual martyrdom.

It had been written in French on thin paper of the kind called India paper at the time. It was paper that easily creased, weighed almost nothing, and could be rolled into a tiny ball and easily swallowed if that were deemed necessary to ensure what was written on it disappeared.

Someone sought to make this letter disappear, although it was undated and unsigned, but not by swallowing it.

It was certainly a startling document for military eyes to scan. Translated, it read :

'Although I have not heard whether you wish to see me I am sending you, sir, some interesting information :

(1) A description of the hydraulic brake of the 120 and how it is operated.
(2) A note on the covering troops. (The new plan contains some changes.)
(3) A note on alterations in artillery formation.
(4) A note relative to Madagascar.
(5) The proposed manual for field artillery (March 14th, 1894).

It has been very difficult to procure the last-named document and I can keep it for only a few days. The Minister has sent a number to the corps, for which they are responsible. Every officer who has one must return it when the manœuvres end. So if you will take what you find useful and have the original ready for me, I will collect it. Unless you prefer that I should copy it *in extenso* and send the copy to you.

I am now leaving to attend the manœuvres.'

Five items of factual military information and an offer to undertake secret copying. It was, however one considered it, a very damaging document, and obviously the work of someone who was prepared to betray the secrets of the French Army to the Germans. Indeed, if this letter was genuine, it meant that there was a paid traitor in France, for presumably such treachery to one's country had to be paid for in favours or cash or both.

Another detail that would interest a knowledgable French Staff officer reading the document was the obvious fact that it had been penned by an artillery officer. The reference to the 120 mm. howitzer in such a familiar manner pointed to this, as did the reference to the artillery manual.

This was the secret letter that was to provide the mystery that turned Alfred Dreyfus into a man living for years without hope in a weakening climate at the other side of the world. In France it became famous by the description given to it. It was known as the *bordereau*, a word that simply meant schedule. But how the *bordereau* came into the hands of Major Henry is part of the much wider Dreyfus mystery. It still has not been satisfactorily explained today.

There was a great deal of speculation on this point later, and what does emerge as surprising is that a large number of high-ranking French officers of the day are understood to have believed that the *bordereau* had been found torn into four pieces, which were covered with other scraps of torn paper in the waste-paper basket in Max von Schwartzkoppen's office in the German Embassy.

The person who found the torn-up *bordereau* and was responsible for removing it was a French charwoman employed at the embassy. She was a Madame Bastian, among whose duties was dusting von Schwartzkoppen's office daily and removing any litter and waste paper. It is not known for certain if Madame Bastian had a second job, one she had not revealed to the secretary at the German Embassy who had hired her services. However, it is very likely that Major Henry, who had some very basic ideas about how to obtain Intelligence information, had contacted her when he knew of her daily job at the embassy and had either frightened her or offered her sufficient cash to be sure she would pass on anything that might be of interest to him.

If this was the case, then Madame Bastian was a spy for French counter-intelligence. It seems amazing that a shrewd person like the German Military Attaché should not have been aware of this. Or if not he, then one of his advisers.

However this may be, the known fact is that the letter torn into quarters arrived at last in Major Henry's office in the Rue Saint-Dominique, where he arranged the pieces in their original order and then pasted them to another sheet of writing paper.

This he took to his superiors.

The result was a bombshell. The message of the *bordereau* apparently confirmed a number of dark suspicions that had been entertained for a considerable time by certain members of the French General Staff, who had insisted for some months past that there was a grave leak and that as a result vital and secret information of a strictly military nature had been passed to the Germans and the Italians.

Now that the *bordereau* had been produced by the Deuxième Bureau these officers openly claimed that Colonel von Schwartzkoppen and the Italian Military Attaché, Colonel Panizzardi, had deliberately employed the services of French traitors.

Major Henry did not have to wait long for the first result of his presenting the *bordereau*. He received instructions to arrange for the Deuxième Bureau's Statistical Section to direct its counter-espionage machinery to trying to uncover who, on the French General Staff, was the mysterious contact used by the German and Italian military attachés.

He employed, at this time, two civilians to go through the waste papers of the suspect embassies, Madame Bastian and a man named Brucker. But he was able to produce no further evidence to be put alongside the notorious *bordereau*. Much later a curious claim, actually made by Dreyfus himself, gave a very different account of how the *bordereau* came into Major Henry's hands. According to this version Madame Bastian was not concerned, and she certainly did not discover the four pieces of thin writing paper in the waste-paper basket, as Major Henry had asserted. The person concerned with discovering the secret letter was Brucker.

The later story, which Dreyfus was to put forward, was that Brucker had become very friendly with the porter at the German Embassy. There was no torn-up letter. What happened was that Brucker persuaded his friend the porter to allow him to enter von Schwartzkoppen's office in the colonel's absence. Left alone, Brucker went through the colonel's secret files and removed the letter.

He took what he had stolen to Major Henry, who, Dreyfus insisted, recognized the handwriting as that of Major Marie Charles Ferdinand Walsin-Esterhazy, a friend of Henry's who was at that time serving with a French infantry regiment. To protect his friend the unhappy Henry tore up the letter, and was on the point of burning the pieces when he was stopped by Brucker, who was well aware of the letter's importance.

'If you destroy this letter, Major Henry,' Brucker said, 'I shall report what happened.'

Henry was a man with no alternative but to reveal the

letter and explain how it came to be torn, so he made up the story which he told to his superior, Colonel Sandherr, who had the pasted-up letter photographed as an aid to discovering whose handwriting was on the torn sheet of paper.

But no one who was shown the letter confidentially recognized the handwriting. A Staff colonel claimed that the letter must have been written by an artillery officer who was a probationer and the only name on the Staff list that met these conditions was that of Captain Alfred Dreyfus.

The name of this colonel was d'Aboville. He was known to be strongly anti-semitic. Because of his insistence his chief, Colonel Fabre, made a report to the War Minister, General Mercier, who was informed that the writing on the *bordereau* resembled that of Dreyfus.

General Mercier asked a handwriting expert employed by the Banque de France, a Monsieur Gobert, to make tests of Dreyfus's handwriting with that in the *bordereau.* Gobert's opinion was not very helpful.

'There is a certain similarity,' he told the War Minister, 'but in my opinion they are not the work of the same hand.'

Mercier next invited the opinion of Alphonse Bertillon, the famous criminologist. Bertillon, whatever his other qualifications, was not a handwriting expert. Believing that a technical opinion was required of him he said he thought the writings were by the same hand. Other so-called experts also agreed with this opinion.

So Dreyfus was summoned to a general inspection, which ended when Major Paty de Clam asked the officer in civilian clothes to take down a letter at his dictation. Dreyfus was actually still writing when he heard the other man say, 'Captain Dreyfus, you are under arrest for high treason.'

The amazed Dreyfus stopped writing and stared in dismay at the speaker, who promptly urged him to confess his guilt in the matter of the *bordereau.* Dreyfus refused indignantly. Whereupon the major drew his Service revolver and placed it on the desk.

'If you wish to use it you will be left alone,' he told Dreyfus.

'I have no reason for using it on myself,' Dreyfus retorted.

'Then I cannot help you,' said the other.

The arrested man was taken to the Cherche-Midi military prison and kept in solitary confinement for three days, during which time his home was searched. Another week dragged past for the arrested man and on October 28th a letter appeared in *Libre Parole* announcing that Captain Dreyfus had been arrested on a charge of espionage. The writer went on : 'The story is that he is travelling, but that is a lie told because they want to hush up the affair. All Israel is stirring.' The writer of the letter signed himself, rather curiously, 'Henry.'

The following day the story was in the national press, and l'Affaire Dreyfus was general knowledge. A court-martial was quickly arranged and opened on December 19th, with Dreyfus's defence undertaken by Maître Charles Demange, a well-known advocate who had been approached by the prisoner's brother Mathieu.

General Mercier had presented to the members of the court-martial documents that had no direct bearing on the case, but were damaging to the defendant. One of these was a letter said to be from von Schwartzkoppen to Colonel Panizzardi which referred to maps of Nice sold to them by 'that rogue D—.' It was readily assumed at the court-martial that the initial stood for Dreyfus. This was incorrect. The man was named Dubois. The prisoner was found guilty on December 22nd and was sentenced to be cashiered from the army and imprisoned for life.

On January 5th 1895, a crowd collected to witness the

Dreyfus cried, 'I am innocent!'

shaming of Alfred Dreyfus in the courtyard of the Ecole Militaire.

'Soldiers,' Dreyfus cried, 'an innocent man is being degraded.' When his sword had been broken he called, 'I am innocent!'

He was handcuffed like a criminal and taken to a civil jail, where he was given a number and photographed. Twelve days later, in the middle of the night, he was taken from Paris. He had begun the first stage of his journey to Devil's Island. After a false report that he had attempted to escape he was ordered to be placed in irons each night. His martyrdom became a bitter experience.

But that lonely man on Devil's Island refused to give up hope that his brother and friends would somehow clear his name.

While he remained there, suffering from the lack of food and comforts, Colonel Picquart, who had been a member of the court-martial, learned that Madame Bastian had in March 1896 removed from von Schwartzkoppen's waste-paper basket the torn pieces of an express letter known as a *petit bleu.*

The colonel was shown this new find, which was addressed to Major Esterhazy by a correspondent who did not sign his name. The letter ran: 'I am awaiting a fuller explanation than you gave me the other day. I beg you to give it me in writing so that I can decide whether to continue my association with House of R.'

Instead of a signature there was the single initial 'C', which was known to be used by the German Military Attaché. Colonel Picquart, who had been very uneasy about Dreyfus's court-martial and the manner in which he had been found guilty and sentenced, had inquiries made about Esterhazy. He learned that the man had wasted his wife's considerable fortune, was in debt, and was being pursued by moneylenders. Even more important was his discovery that the German Military Staff had been amazed by the trial and sentencing of Alfred Dreyfus. They had never heard of him. So obviously he could not be the mysterious 'D—' of the letter produced at the court-martial, which had influenced the verdict. Picquart, a fair-minded man, came to the conclusion that Dreyfus had been convicted unjustly. He was also a man of action. He approached General de Boisdeffre and showed him the evidence he had uncovered. The General Staff's chief scented more scandal in Picquart's discoveries and turned the colonel over to his deputy, General Gonse, who immediately ordered that there should be no linking of Esterhazy's name with the Dreyfus case.

Picquart was not impressed. 'There may have been a mistrial, General,' he pointed out. 'The honour of the French Army is involved.'

Gonse's sour reply was, 'We can't reopen the Dreyfus case.'

A little later Picquart was transferred to duties in Tunisia. Obviously to get rid of a man who could be an embarrassment to the officers of the General Staff. However, before he left the colonel related his findings and fears to a lawyer named Leblois, who discussed the new developments with some members of the Senate.

Major Henry had by this time been promoted to colonel, and he was not idle during the time Picquart was busy. He claimed to have found yet another letter, from the Italian Military Attaché, Colonel Panizzardi. Its contents seemed to confirm the guilt of the lonely man on Devil's Isle, who was certainly being more keenly remembered than many people in Paris desired. The new letter proved to be a forgery. So plainly there were interests working to keep Dreyfus away from France, in the hope that he and the story of the *bordereau* would be forgotten in time. But the prisoner's brother sent a letter to the Minister. This he also had published in the newspapers. He accused Esterhazy of being a spy and author of the *bordereau.*

Suddenly the Dreyfus case exploded with bomb-like effect. There was a demand for action in the press and Esterhazy was court-martialled. But just as too much evidence was produced at the trial of Dreyfus by his brother officers, so too little was presented at the trial of Esterhazy. There was no mention of Colonel Picquart or his findings. Esterhazy was acquitted.

Two days later the brilliant writer Emile Zola published in the newspaper *L'Aurore* a letter addressed to the President of France. That letter was to become world famous. It was headed '*J'Accuse.*' In it he accused the members of the December 1894 court-martial with breaking the law by using secret evidence and concealing other evidence that should have been public.

The scent of scandal, so feared by de Boisdeffre, had become an unpleasant reek that was spreading throughout France. Zola and the editor of *L'Aurore*, whose name was Perreux, were accused in a counter-claim of defaming the members of the court-martial, whom Zola had named. Major Paty de Clam, another who had been promoted to colonel, had also received dishonourable mention by Zola. Zola and Perreux were brought to trial, and the hearing lasted from February 7th until the 23rd. After that time the jury produced a verdict of guilty and Zola called them cannibals. He was sentenced to a year's imprisonment and a fine of three thousand francs. The same fine was imposed on his publisher, who was jailed for four months. The two men appealed and the Appeal Court set aside the verdict of guilty and ordered a second trial. Zola crossed to England, where he remained until 1899, when the Dreyfus case was finally reopened, the object for which he had taken great personal risk.

Behind him in France he left the country full of excitement. What was the truth? Why should there be any mystery? These were the questions all shades of French opinion demanded should be answered promptly. The uneasy General Staff had a private inquiry. It was presided over by the two generals, de Boisdeffre and Gonse, who had feared scandal. Under close questioning Colonel Henry broke down and admitted forging the 'rogue D—' letter, substituting the initial for the name Dubois. He was arrested, but committed suicide in his prison cell.

General de Boisdeffre resigned his post and Colonel Paty de Clam was dismissed from the Army.

The climate was changing. At least Esterhazy thought this, and escaped while he could. Like Zola, he crossed to England. Unlike Zola, he never returned to France. He remained in England until he died in Harpenden in 1923. However, in this changed climate Madame Dreyfus was able to petition the Cour de Cassation for a formal reconsideration of her husband's case. Early in 1899 the Criminal Division of the Appeal Court consented, and Zola came back to France, aware that he had helped to make the Dreyfus affair one of great interest throughout the world.

On June 9th Alfred Dreyfus, thin and ill, started the journey back to France. This time he was not taken aboard the black-hulled convict ship *Martinier*. A grey cruiser of the French Navy had been sent to bring him back to his homeland. On July 1st he stepped ashore and was transported to Rennes. His new trial, which was expected to clear him, opened in the capital of Brittany in September. France waited for his release, and was shocked when the court sitting under Colonel Jouast found that Dreyfus was guilty but declared that due to circumstances, the sentence should be reduced. The officers who voted for the verdict had a majority of five to two. The prisoner's sentence was changed to ten years' imprisonment.

When the fresh court's finding was published an outcry rose throughout the entire country, and the Government of the day became fearful of the public's demand for true justice and displeasure with the members of the General Staff. There was only one way to show the disapproval of the General Staff's attitude. President Loubet took it. He gave Dreyfus the equivalent of a free pardon.

General de Gallifret, the Minister of War at the time, tried to take refuge behind the President's order and declared the Dreyfus case closed.

He was to be proved wrong, for Dreyfus wrote a book he entitled *Five Years of My Life*, which told the truth about the harsh and at times terrible conditions of his life on Devil's Island. In the book he inquired why he should be pardoned for a crime he had not committed.

Neither the Government nor the Army had anyone prepared to give him an answer. So the work of seeking the truth continued under the leadership and encouragement of men like Zola, who died shortly before new facts could be presented to the authorities in 1903. Even after this it took another three years of the Cour de Cassation to set aside the verdict of the second court, which had sat at Rennes. This time the decision was not a majority one. It was unanimous.

Belatedly the Government sought to make amends. Dreyfus was promoted to major and decorated with the Cross of Chevalier of the Legion of Honour. At the same time Picquart, who had in the meanwhile been dismissed for his support of the prisoner on Devil's Isle, was reinstated and promoted to brigadier-general.

The Dreyfus case at last was closed, but the mystery which surrounded it and the fight to achieve justice for a much-wronged man have remained a constant reminder throughout the twentieth century of how prejudice and misplaced loyalty can be dangerous weapons in the hands of men who have no clear idea of justice and the rights of others.

Dreyfus died in 1935 after an illness that had its origin in the suffering he had undergone in French Guiana. It took another decade of criticism and public disfavour before the notorious Devil's Island was finally closed by a special commission sent from France.

That closure was the final attempt to make up for sufferings of Alfred Dreyfus, whose loneliness on the island had drawn the eyes of the world to that piece of rock another Frenchman had described as the 'dry guillotine'.

9

The Mystery of Anastasia

For more than half a century various claims have been made that the youngest daughter of the ill-fated Czar Nicholas of Russia survived in 1918 the massacre of her family in Ekaterinburg. Not only that, but various claimants have from time to time come forward over that period of fifty years to announce that they were the Grand Duchess Anastasia.

Most of them were surrounded by mystery. Nearly all of them had an interesting story to tell. But none of them succeeded in convincing all who listened that Anastasia had indeed returned to the world that had considered her dead.

As late as August 1970 the survival of Anastasia at the time of the massacre was again news throughout the world, when Prince Alexis, a descendant of the unfortunate Romanoff family, came forward with yet another claim to knowing the truth of what happened in Ekaterinburg in July 1918. He wrote a letter to the French newspaper *Le Figaro* in which he stated that his grandfather, Prince Nicholas Romanoff-Dolgorouky, was with the White Russian troops fighting the Bolsheviks in Latvia in 1918. By the fortunes of war he was thrown into the company of a Red Army officer named Vazetis.

As can be the custom, even between fighting men in armies opposed to each other, the prince and the Red Army soldier talked about their different experiences and exchanged confidences. Comrade Vazetis had been an assistant to Trotsky, who with Lenin had made the successful October revolution of 1917 possible and victory a certainty.

According to the prince, writing in the Paris newspaper, his grandfather had asked the Soviet officer if it were true that, as rumour had it, the royal family had been machine-gunned in a cellar in a house in the Ukraine. A great many persons could not believe that such a slaughter had been ordered as a matter of policy by the new masters of Russia.

According to Vazetis the Ekaterinburg massacre had been admitted by Trotsky, whom he had heard say, 'The whole family was liquidated, but in Moscow they are annoyed because one of the children was saved.'

There was an enlargement of this. Prince Alexis said that his grandfather had escaped the civil war in Russia and some years later, when he met Queen Marie of Rumania, Prince Nicholas had mentioned the story about the child who had escaped. She had been very interested and said she would ask the Rumanian police to make enquiries.

It was as a result of this Rumanian police investigation that a report was made to Queen Marie that, early in 1919, two old men and an elderly woman, who were taking care of a sick girl, had entered Rumania from Russia. They had apparently made the journey in secret, taking care to avoid arousing the notice of the Soviet police. The girl's sickness had apparently been due to early privations and not receiving proper medical care and sufficient nutritious food. The Rumanian police questioned the grown-ups and asked who was this girl accompanying them.

They had looked at each other and the woman had broken into tears and said in a sobbing voice, 'She is the Grand Duchess Anastasia.'

This story told to Prince Alexis' grandfather by Queen Marie had been written into Prince Nicholas' memoirs. These had not been published, but the manuscript remained hidden away in a locked safe.

As a footnote to this statement Prince Alexis added that confirmation that the little grand duchess had been saved that day in Ekaterinburg had come from Prince Yussupov, the man who had arranged the late-night party which had been attended by Rasputin to meet his murderers. Prince Yussupov had met Prince Alexis shortly before the former's death, and on that occasion had confided that he knew for certain the Grand Duchess Anastasia was alive.

What prompted the letter to *Le Figaro* by Prince Alexis? One cannot be sure, but it may be considered a contributing factor that not long before, after a round of legal battles that had been waged for not far short of forty years, a court in Germany had officially rejected an appeal by a Mrs. John Manahan, formerly known as Anna Anderson, who had insisted she was the missing Anastasia.

Mrs. John Manahan had been the latest claimant to be rejected after investigation of the claim she had put forward. But her claim had served to keep the mystery surrounding Anastasia and what happened to the girl in a cellar echoing to the sound of gunfire very much alive.

The person who had first given rise to the story that the Grand Duchess Anastasia Nikolaievna had survived and escaped from the cellar was a certain Madame Tchaikowsky. Until she appeared mysteriously and suddenly in Berlin it had been generally supposed throughout the world that Anastasia had perished with the others of the doomed Czar's family when the shooting started in the dark and was kept up until all the royal prisoners had fallen. Certainly the bodies in the cellar had been left lying there for a considerable time afterwards.

Madame Tchaikowsky was a personable woman who contacted Prince Constantine Gabriel, the acknowledged leader of the Czarist refugees living in the German capital after escaping from Russia, and later was by him introduced to Gleb Botkin, whose father had been Court physician to the Russian Imperial family.

In a private interview with Botkin, Madame Tchaikowsky made what seemed to him at the time an incredible claim. The son of the dead Czar's physician asked time to consider what he had been told.

However, in some way the story and its secret was leaked to others in the Russian refugee colony in Berlin, and shortly afterwards the story was being spread throughout Europe that on that fatal day in July 1918 not all the Czar's family had died under the fire of the murderers who shot in the dark so that their faces could not be seen.

Someone had lived and escaped. The girl Anastasia had been taken from that dark cellar of death and secretly hidden, then smuggled away from the town and helped to make her way across a homeland that had become enemy country to her.

The next development was the attaching of a name to the person who claimed to be the rescued Anastasia. She was Madame Tchaikowsky.

After that the full story was released with the approval of Prince Constantine Gabriel, and for a very good reason. Both he and Gleb Botkin had finally accepted the mysterious newcomer to Berlin as the genuine grand duchess.

Her claim was quite sensational.

According to Madame Tchaikowsky, her escape in July 1918 had been contrived by a Russian soldier who had no sympathy with the orders given to him and his comrades to murder the royal family. After the gunfire had ceased he had crept into the cellar where the corpses lay as they had been shot down and examined them in turn. He had found Anastasia wounded but alive. He had cautioned her to keep silent, and had taken her from the cellar and concealed her until he could desert. He knew he would not be sought very strenuously, for it was a time when food was desperately short in a land that had gone through a terrible revolution and civil war and where the peasants were refusing to tend the blood-soaked soil. Every day soldiers were deserting and returning home, anxious about their families and possessions. In the country districts all was confusion.

This alone had made it possible for the soldier to make his way towards the Rumanian border with the disguised girl.

There might have been something else urging him to get out of Russia. This was the fact that, according to Madame Tchaikowsky, the rescued girl had sewn into her clothes some very valuable emeralds. How they had come to be there or who had stitched the gems into the clothes she could not say. But they were found by the Russian soldier after he and the girl had been living a hand-to-mouth existence for some time.

They had reached Bucharest, where the soldier, whose name was Tchaikowsky, later married the girl he had rescued and brought out of Russia. They had lived with no one knowing the young wife's true identity. But Trotsky, after being told that Anastasia was missing when the bodies were taken from the cellar, had sent members of the new Soviet Secret Police to track down the soldier who had been reporter as a deserter.

The men sent to find what had happened to the missing daughter of the Czar had finally succeeded in trailing the fugitives to Bucharest, where a trap had been set. Only the soldier had walked into it. His wife had not been with him when Trotsky's agents attempted to repair the error made at Ekaterinburg, of not ensuring that all the royal family were dead when the firing stopped. He had died, and his young widow had escaped, determined to reach another country, where she would be safe from further pursuit and violence.

For this reason Madame Tchaikowsky had gone to Berlin, where she knew there was a considerable colony of Russian refugees.

In the German capital she had succeeded in convincing Prince Constantine and Botkin that she was the person she claimed to be.

So the full story was released.

However, to be released was not to be accepted. There were many sceptics in the Russian colony, and almost overnight the refugees were divided into two groups : those who accepted Madame Tchaikowsky as the genuine Grand Duchess Anastasia, and those who claimed she was a fake. But acceptance and support by Prince Constantine and Botkin proved to be all the pretender could wish. Gradually she came to be accepted as the real Anastasia, which meant she was given a place at the head of the Russian colony in Berlin.

There still remained some doubters, who were quite vocal, and these included a number of persons who corresponded regularly with Grand Duke Cyril and Grand Duke Boris, both members of the Romanoff family.

The subject of Anastasia and Madame Tchaikowsky's claim became so bitter in time that a way had to be found of proving Madame Tchaikowsky was indeed the Grand Duchess Anastasia beyond reasonable doubt. This became particularly necessary when a rumour spread throughout Berlin that Madame Tchaikowsky had been prevented from committing suicide by throwing herself from a bridge over the River Spree. Almost every story related about Madame Tchaikowsky was sensational.

The reason for the attempted suicide, if that was indeed what had been planned, was the woman's bitter frustration at having doubts continue about her true status. It was said to have affected her mind.

Not surprisingly this won a good deal of additional sympathy for a person of the background claimed by Madame Tchaikowsky. Prince Constantine told Botkin he should resolve everyone's doubts by making a formal declaration of acceptance.

As the prince pointed out, Botkin had actually known the youngest daughter of the Czar.

'So you can't be mistaken,' he insisted.

'The Grand Duchess Anastasia was only seven years old, you must remember, when I met her with my father,' Botkin reminded the prince.

'And how old were you?' Prince Constantine inquired.

'Eight.'

'But there's nothing wrong with your memory?'

'Nothing.'

On the strength of this childhood meeting Gleb Botkin made the formal statement accepting Madame Tchaikowsky. There could be no criticism of Botkin's sincerity, but he was known to be very much under the influence of Prince Constantine. More impartial members of the Russian colony in Berlin strove to provide their own proof that the grand duchess had returned to her own people. There was in Germany at the time a woman who had been a nurse to several members of the Czar's family. This woman was known as Sascha, and her claim to being the royal family's nurse at one time was never questioned. Long before Madame Tchaikowsky appeared in Berlin it was widely known that Sascha had attended the Grand Duchess Anastasia.

Sascha was brought to Berlin and a meeting arranged for her to be confronted by Madame Tchaikowsky. This too proved to be another sensational event.

The room was crowded when Sascha entered, looked round at the many faces, and at once went to where Madame Tchaikowsky sat and fell upon her knees, saying excitedly, 'Oh, Your Imperial Highness!'

Sascha fell upon her knees . . .

There was sudden silence in that room, as though all the on-lookers were holding their breath. Madame Tchaikowsky rose and raised the crouching nurse to her feet.

'I am truly delighted to see you again, dear Zhura,' said Madame Tchaikowsky, smiling.

There was a sound like hissing as watchers took a fresh and deep breath, and tears were seen gleaming in many eyes. Zhura was the pet name the little Anastasia had given Sascha in bygone days in St. Petersburg. There was suddenly a great deal more hissing, or so it seemed, in that room. It was really the sound of a large assembly of people breathing a collective sigh of relief.

Madame Tchaikowsky had been accepted by her old nurse. Anastasia had indeed returned.

When this meeting between the former nurse and the woman who had addressed her by her familiar name in the royal household was reported in the newspapers it produced an unexpected reaction which dismayed those who had accepted Madame Tchaikowsky as the genuine Anastasia. The two Romanoff grand dukes, Boris and Cyril, refused to accept Madame Tchaikowsky.

'She is an impostor,' they maintained. 'Anastasia died in 1918.'

There developed a bitter correspondence between the two Czarist factions, pro and con the newly appeared Anastasia, and the confusion was not mended when a certain Captain Djamgaroff took a middle course by proclaiming, 'It has not been fully proved who Madame Tchaikowsky is. But there can be no doubt that she is insane, suffering from a persecution mania with its customary symptom—the delusion of grandeur.'

Doubtless the captain was stating no more than a sincere belief, but his words did nothing to resolve a notable historical mystery. Rather otherwise. It served to harden the opposed opinions.

This condition of stalemate continued for seven years, during which time the mystery was hotly debated not only throughout Europe, but in America. However, there was no notable development until Frau von Ratieff's memoirs appeared with a startling claim that Grand Duke Boris and Grand Duke Cyril were involved in a scheme to have Madame Tchaikowsky's claim discredited. After giving her own reasons for accepting Madame Tchaikowsky as the genuine Anastasia, Frau von Ratieff enlarged her exposé to explain that the reason why the pair of grand dukes opposed Prince Constantine Gabriel was that, by admitting Anastasia had returned, they would have endangered their own positions as heads of the Romanoff family, positions that entitled them to have the use of certain funds and properties placed at the royal family's disposal by a number of persons who had made offerings to the dead Czar's memory.

This volume of memoirs revived the entire question of whether Anastasia had really survived the slaughter in the Ekaterinburg cellar. The fresh bitterness of the opposed Czarist factions could only be resolved by proof. The question became, how could such proof be obtained?

Some of the less traditional seekers of the truth decided to make an appeal to Professor Gilliard in Lausanne, Switzerland, in the hope that science could help them with their difficulty. This approach to the professor was made in January 1927. He decided to take up the problem with the Director of the Institute of Scientific Police, Mark Bischoff, who was duly supplied with a collection of photographs of both the Grand Duchess Anastasia and of Madame Tchaikowsky.

Bischoff agreed to make detailed comparisons as he might in a case involving the criminal courts. He little realized how much world-wide publicity this decision was to bring him, not all of it desirable.

He had his staff take fresh photographs of the profiles of the two women, using the original photographs supplied by Professor Gilliard, with special attention paid to the subjects' ears. These new profile portraits were made at a scale precisely proportional to each other. The basic measurement was to be the length of a subject's face from the exact centre of the eyebrows to the bottom of the chin. The extreme length of the ears were measured in proportion to the face. These two measurements were for fundamental references in relative likeness. They were obtained in the institute's photographic laboratory by twice arranging the different profiles reproduced to exact scale in the way in which two heads are arranged for stamping profiles on commemoration medallions, that is, both facing in the same direction, with one profile above and slightly behind the other.

In the first reproduction Anastasia's head was uppermost, in the second Madame Tchaikowsky's. In this way it was possible to emphasize differences in detail in the two profiles. Such differences were particularly noticeable in the nose structures. However, such differences could not be taken as conclusive because the passage of years and even a change of personal habits might account for them, at least in part. Bischoff decided to concentrate on an ear.

He chose Anastasia's right ear, which was reproduced from two photographs, one taken in 1912, six years before the shooting in the cellar, and the other not very long before the massacre in Ekaterinburg. He found that both ears in these guaranteed photographs revealed the same narrowness at the outer edge and a wide area in the top half with only a suggestion of convolution of folding.

In short, these two right ears, one photographed after an interval of six years, were shown to be identical.

On the other hand, when Madame Tchaikowsky's right ear was reproduced for comparison, it was found to differ considerably in basic shape. The outside edge was not so narrow. In fact, it was much more prominent, and the convolutions covered a much wider area than in the Anastasia ear.

With his visual evidence to support him, Bischoff informed Professor Gillard that Madame Tchaikowsky could not possibly be the Grand Duchess Anastasia.

The laboratory work had taken eight months. In that time other photographs of members of the dead Czar's family were similarly compared with photographs of Madame Tchaikowsky. This additional work convinced Bischoff that there were no positive family resemblances at all between the Romanoffs and the woman claiming to be the Czar's youngest daughter.

When the Lausanne findings were announced Madame Tchaikowsky felt a cold wind of change blowing about her in Berlin. She decided to leave Europe. She sailed for the United States in the *Berengaria*. She used another name and scarcely moved outside her cabin during the voyage. But her flight, if that was what her journey really was, did not remain the secret she had hoped to keep it. When the liner docked she found newsmen and photographers waiting for her to step down the gang-plank. She tried to avoid the cameras and would not answer the questions put to her by reporters.

However, the next editions of the New York newspapers announced that Madame Tchaikowsky, who had claimed to be the Grand Duchess Anastasia of Russia, had arrived from Europe as the guest of Mrs. William B. Leeds, a well-known American hostess and socialite who before her marriage had been the Russian Princess Xenia.

Madame Tchaikowsky was again the centre of a great deal of world interest. Knowing of the findings in Lausanne, some American editors sent Bischoff copies of a formal photograph distributed by Madame Tchaikowsky to the press after she had joined Mrs. Leeds. The Lausanne laboratory was asked to make further comparisons with the new photos.

Bischoff agreed, and the result was a great surprise for him and his staff. The new photos showed that Madame Tchaikowsky and the Grand Duchess Anastasia had identical right ears! This change had come about after an interval of only a few months. Bischoff issued an abrasive comment on the new photos. He said, 'From this evidence the alleged portrait of Madame Tchaikowsky appearing in the *New York Evening Post* of February 7th, 1928, is a retouched reproduction of the photograph of the Grand Duchess Anastasia Nikolaievna.'

This time there was no counter-claim from Madame Tchaikowsky. Science had worsted her and she was completely discredited. She merged into obscurity, her last frail pretence swept away.

But her emergence on a stage where she was seen by the entire world had served to rouse a great interest in the truth of what really did happen to the Czar's youngest daughter. When she had vanished from the stage the interest in Anastasia remained. Indeed, so great was the interest in this mystery that Hollywood set out to provide its own solution in a film.

The film used a good deal of the story that was familiar to Czarist refugees in Berlin and other cities throughout Europe that had offered the displaced Russian nobility a haven after the Bolsheviks had swept to victory. Many of the sequences in that story were shot on sets where the returned Anastasia met former friends who claimed to identify her. The episode with the nurse was not omitted. It was made into the turning point of the story.

But when the film was shown there were Russian nobles driving taxis in the streets of Paris who laughed at it. There were others who frowned when they saw it, for unquestionably Madame Tchaikowsky had vanished only to leave behind her a legend. The legend was surrounded by mystery.

For instance, could the elderly woman who had been nurse to the Romanoffs have been mistaken in her instant recognition of the woman the grand dukes branded an impostor without seeing her? But if Sascha had made a genuine mistake, what of Madame Tchaikowsky's calling her by the familiar name belonging to the former days in St. Petersburg?

There have been a number of suggestions, none of them kind to the woman claiming to be Anastasia. It was said that she had been aided by friends of Prince Constantine Gabriel and Gleb Botkin, persons who had known of certain characteristics of Anastasia who had passed these on to a woman who was no more than an actress playing a part for rather high stakes—her share of the fortune controlled by the grand dukes.

Certainly Bischoff had no hesitation in branding the woman who had handed out a fake photo of herself to New York pressmen as an impostor.

On that much firmer basis one can discount Madame Tchaikowsky's claim to be Anastasia.

But the legend continues, because it remains today and has flourished for half a century, but soon it will be too late for further pretenders to come forward unless they are very old and with little hope of telling why they have remained in the shadows for so many years.

For what one cannot discount is the belief held by persons in a position to know the truth that Anastasia did escape from the cellar of death and remain uncaptured by the Bolsheviks, who would have seen no advantage to the new regime in Russia in keeping alive a constant reminder of what had happened in Ekaterinburg. But if Anastasia did vanish, where did she vanish to? She must have had help. Who offered her aid?

For instance, the statement in late 1970 by Prince Alexis that Yussupov had confided to him that Anastasia was still alive cannot be ignored. Prince Felix Yussupov, at the time of his plot to kill Rasputin in 1916, was married to the Czar's niece, the Grand Duchess Irina, then considered to be the most beautiful woman in Russia. One of the conspirators who joined Yussupov's plot to rid Russia of the notorious Staretz, as Rasputin was known to his dupes, was another member of the royal family, the Grand Duke Nicholas, while the Czar's cousin, Grand Duke Dimitri Pavlovich, was another active member who loaned his car to the murderers on the night Rasputin was slain.

Yussupov up to the time of his death was in contact with most of the Romanoff survivors of the Bolshevik Revolution. If he claimed Anastasia was alive it was likely that he believed he had ample reason for making the claim.

In that case the real mystery lies in the true Anastasia's refusal to come forward and proclaim herself to the many supporters of a lost cause who would have received her with joy and enthusiasm. For that was what, for many years, the Russian refugees were living for—the day when Anastasia would return to place herself at their head and they would be a real royalist community again.

True, there is a certain dreamlike quality to the situation. There is little reality in it, for no believer in Anastasia's escape had claimed to give the whole story or to offer facts that spelled conviction.

The story told by Queen Marie was undoubtedly believed by her. But were the Rumanian police who made the investigation mistaken? If they were not, where did the trail of known facts end? What prevented Queen Marie from publishing the discoveries of the Rumanian police?

There are so many unanswered questions that the mystery grows the more one considers it. However, there could be a simple answer to most of them if Anastasia did escape. Her appalling experience in the dark cellar, with her family being slaughtered around her like cattle, may have affected her in such a way that she refused to return to a world where such events could happen. She may have insisted on living without recognition, being an ordinary woman who could pass her days without fear of the Soviet Secret Police seeking her and completing what was left undone at Ekaterinburg.

For if Trotsky had indeed told his assistant Vazetis that one of the Czar's children was saved he would have had proof. Trotsky was never a man to deal in half-truths.

But now that the German courts have disallowed the Manahan appeal for recognition it seems very unlikely that any more claimants will come forward. Of several who appeared after Madame Tchaikowsky's disappearance none was accepted. None even achieved her degree of success. She had known so much to support her claim that in her case the real mystery is, rather, who aided her and schooled her in her fake role? According to the Rumanian police Anastasia had crossed the Rumanian frontier. Madame Tchaikowsky had come from Bucharest, the Rumanian capital. Had a plot been prepared in that city, perhaps by someone with knowledge of what the police had reported to Queen Marie?

It is at least a possibility. Which is the most one can say today for that claim that Anastasia escaped from Ekaterinburg and was not buried with her father and the others of her murdered family.

10

The Expedition that Vanished

On a moist April evening in 1824 two sisters named Griffin were invited to dine with Captain John Franklin and his wife at their home. A number of other naval captains were present for the occasion, most of whom had a keen eye for a pretty woman. Jane Griffin was unquestionably the prettiest woman present, and it was in acknowledgment of this that she was seated next to the host. Over the meal her sister Fanny spoke to a rather gruff guest named Captain Parry who was in high favour at the Admiralty.

She said, 'Captain Franklin has a very fine head. Don't you agree, Captain Parry?'

The somewhat surprised man beside her turned to look at the speaker. His teeth showed through his whiskers in a quick smile of amusement.

'Yes indeed, Miss Griffin,' he agreed. 'In fact, it is the finest head I know.' He paused, holding her with his amused but approving gaze. 'Inside as well as out,' he added, leaning closer and dropping his voice.

Four years later, after his wife's death, John Franklin married the lovely Jane. By this time he was a man marked out for high honours and success, as Jane Griffin realized in the following year when, her husband having received a knighthood, she became Lady Franklin.

She went with him to Tasmania when he had been appointed the island's lieutenant-governor, but unfortunately it was her interest in all her husband did and her keenness to further his career that caused argument among his staff and he was summoned back to England. He considered he had been unjustly treated and gave up hope of working in future under the Colonial Office. Instead, he gave his mind to Arctic exploration, a subject then being discussed in London at gatherings where he found old companions and kindred spirits.

Five years before, in 1838, James Ross had recommended to the Council of the Royal Geographical Society an expedition to discover the legendary north-west Passage, a seaway which was believed to run from the north Atlantic to the north Pacific and the idea of which had fascinated explorers since the days of Hawkins and Frobisher. Ross' idea had been passed over in favour of an expedition to undertake a magnetic survey of the Antarctic. Now, within a few months of Franklin's return to England, Ross' proposal was put forward again after being approved by the Royal Society.

This time the plan received the Admiralty's approval and was later backed by Sir Robert Peel, who was Prime Minister. The matter of a commander for the new expedition was debated, and it is believed that a letter sent by Lady Franklin to Ross won the latter's support for her husband. This support had influence at the Admiralty and Sir John Franklin was in due course informed by the Admiralty that he had been appointed to command the expedition.

In her letter to Sir James Ross, Lady Franklin had written, 'I dread exceedingly the effect on his mind of being without honourable and immediate employment, and it is this which enables me to support the idea of parting with him on a service of difficulty and danger better than I otherwise should.'

The former Jane Griffin had little idea when she spoke of her personal dread that she was helping to further her husband's appointment to a command which would take him to his death and result in one of the most famous mysteries in the history of exploration.

News that the expedition was preparing created a great deal of enthusiasm and excitement in the British Isles, and when Franklin announced, 'No service is nearer to my heart than the completion of the survey of the north coast of America and the accomplishment of a north-west passage,' he was hailed as a hero and empire-builder in the popular mould of the mid-nineteenth century.

By that time British explorers had already achieved much in the Arctic, some of them doubtless spurred by the knowledge that a century earlier, in 1745, the British Government of the day had offered a prize of twenty thousand pounds to any explorer who discovered 'a north-west passage through Hudson's Strait to the western and southern oceans of America.'

In the year Franklin received his most memorable command a ship had yet to sail by a northern route from the Atlantic to the Pacific. Enthusiasm for Franklin's expedition, during the time preparations for it were made, became so general in Britain that the outcome was awaited with every confidence by the ordinary man in the street.

Franklin himself was fifty-nine, a naval captain of considerable experience, and his reputation had an almost magnetic quality, for applications to join the expedition in any way poured into the Admiralty from all sections and classes of the community. However, his age was considered a possible drawback by some cautious minds, though not by Franklin himself.

When the First Lord of the Admiralty, Lord Haddington, asked him in friendly fashion, 'Have you really thought seriously of the nature of this undertaking at your age? For you see, I know your age—you are fifty-nine,' Franklin's reply was typical of the man.

'Not quite, my lord,' he corrected Haddington.

He was two months from his fifty-ninth birthday.

The First Lord continued to make his point. 'I feel a great responsibility in this matter,' he confided to Franklin. 'If you were to break down I should be blamed for having sent so old a man.'

He was giving the enthusiastic Franklin a chance for second thoughts in case the man had secret fears for his health. Franklin had no such fears.

'If I did not think myself equal to the task,' he maintained stoutly. 'I should not wish to go.'

There was no objection after that.

The ships chosen for the expedition were the *Erebus* and the *Terror*. Both vessels had been specially fitted out for work in the Polar regions, with bows and sterns strengthened with solid baulks of timber to withstand the pressure of the ice-pack. They were given distinctive colours—black hulls, white masts, and yellow superstructures. The *Erebus*, which was to be Franklin's flagship, was a vessel of three hundred and seventy tons. The *Terror*, to be commanded by Captain F. R. M. Crozier, who had sailed in her before, was slightly smaller. Her tonnage was three hundred and twenty-six. Under Franklin but in command of *Erebus* was another distinguished sailor, Captain James Fitzjames. Each of the two ships carried sixty-seven officers and men, so that the expedition mounted a total of twenty-three officers and one hundred and eleven men.

The instructions Franklin received before leaving England were to sail through the Davis Strait and along the coast of Greenland and then to turn westward and make his way through Lancaster Sound and Barrow Strait as far as Cape Walker. This was the extreme edge of North Somerset Island. From here he would be a man entering the unknown. He was to make the best of his way southward and westward in an effort to find that long-sought channel that for hundreds of years had been a legendary north-west Passage in which generations of Artic explorers had believed without having the fortune to discover it. When he had found this legendary stretch of water Franklin was to navigate it and then make for the Bering Strait, which would allow him to pass into the Pacific.

Because he was a man of experience, Franklin had an alternative plan prepared should he not find the channel when sailing on a south-west course after leaving Cape Walker. He would face his ships about and take a northern course through the Wellington Channel, which was on the north of Barrow strait. However, he did not doubt that the more southerly course would reveal the channel he sought.

He was prepared to spend some years on the expedition and took supplies to last for three years which could if necessary be rationed to extend to four.

Lady Franklin made the Union Jack her husband was to take with him. It is said that he sat watching her make the last stitches in the drawing-room of their home in Brook Street, off Grosvenor Square, and that when she put down her needle she rose and with a happy cry threw it over him.

'Finished at last,' she said excitedly.

Her husband surprised her by jumping to his feet and snatching the flag away from his head and shoulders.

'Jane!' he said in a shocked voice. 'What have you done? You must know that the Union Jack is used as a shroud for those buried at sea!'

Like most deep-water sailormen, John Franklin had not lived through his career without achieving some degree of superstition.

Although not a superstitious woman, Lady Franklin felt suddenly fearful. She was to remember that moment for most of her life.

On the 19th of May the *Erebus* and the *Terror* weighed anchor at Greenhithe on the Thames and sailed with the turning tide for the North Sea. The expedition continued north of Scotland and called at Stromness in the Orkneys, where they stayed for two days before heading westward across the Atlantic in blustery weather. On Midsummer Day the two little ships rounded the extreme southern point of Greenland, Cape Farewell, and the next day were threading their way through drifting icebergs. Nine days later, on July 4th, they dropped anchor off Whalefish Island, in Disko Bay, on Greenland's west coast.

A transport vessel had accompanied *Erebus* and *Terror* thus far on the journey. At the anchorage off Whalefish Island the extra stores carried by the transport were taken aboard the other two ships, and the transport made ready to return to England, carrying letters for home written by the members of the expedition and five who had gone down sick and were being sent back. Among the mail taken aboard the transport was Franklin's last letter to his wife. It was cheerful and encouraging in tone and the writer sounded confident about the expedition's outcome. Almost as though recalling the episode of the Union Jack in the Brook Street drawing-room, Franklin told his wife she must not have 'the slightest apprehension' about him, even if the expedition had to be away for two winters.

Three days after he had written that letter *Erebus* and *Terror* were again sailing north, this time heading for Melville Bay, where on July 26th they actually made fast to a drifting iceberg, on which a temporary observatory was constructed. The next stage of the voyage was across Baffin Bay to Lancaster Sound, where they were joined by a whaler from Hull. This was the *Prince of Wales*. Her skipper, Captain Dannet, was probably the last man to see the Franklin expedition before it vanished in Lancaster Sound. He remained watching the ships through his spyglass until they disappeared.

After that day there was only silence from the crews that

had set out from Greenhithe in such high spirits and with soaring hopes for what the expedition would accomplish.

For many months no word was expected, and 1845 passed, then 1846, and finally the spring of 1847, by which time word of the expedition's outcome should certainly have been received in Britain. Friends of Franklin and his men became worried, and before long the first suggestion of a relief expedition to find the lost ships was made.

True, before the Franklin expedition had sailed there had been an understanding that the Admiralty would request the Hudson's Bay Company to release emergency supplies for the expedition at some of their northernmost trading posts. As a result fishing tackle had been forwarded to posts on the Mackenzie River and on Great Slave Lake. Also, Eskimos had been told to keep a look out for the two ships in the Mackenzie and Coppermine country. No trading post reported the expedition's arrival, no Eskimo claimed to have seen the ships.

H.M.S. *Erebus* and H.M.S. *Terror* had sailed into the unknown and vanished.

By the autumn of 1847 Lady Franklin was seeking advice about a possible relief expedition to find the lost explorers. She offered most of her personal money and that of her husband to help finance such a search for the missing men. It was not until some months later, in 1848, that the Admiralty approached the commissioners of Customs and Excise with the request that British whaling crews try to find news of the missing expedition. Various sums were suggested as payment for any whaling captain who brought positive news.

No whaler captain returned with news that was worth following up, and it was not until later that same year the Admiralty became convinced that it had to send a fresh expedition to discover what had happened to the first—if it could.

In actual fact it sent two expeditions. One consisted of two ships under the command of Captain Sir James Clarke Ross. These ships were the *Enterprise* and the *Investigator.* They were to follow after Franklin's ships in the hope of providing an answer to the mystery of their disappearance. The second expedition was commanded by a friend of Franklin's, Sir John Richardson, who was accompanied by Dr. John Rae. They were to examine the nothern coast-line of America, while two other vessels, the *Plover* and the *Herald*, were to continue through the Bering Strait until they joined up with Richardson's party.

These relief parties did not leave until 1848. They were back in England a year later with nothing to report. By this time the fate of the Franklin expedition and the mystery of what had happened to it had become a subject that caused a great many people in Britain to demand a more vigorous approach to finding a solution.

In response to public clamour the Government offered a reward of ten thousand pounds for what it described as 'first information of the fate of the Franklin expedition.' Lady Franklin offered an additional three thousand pounds. As a direct result of these offers, by the autumn of 1850 fifteen ships were in the Arctic trying to solve the mystery.

Lady Franklin, desperate to leave no stone unturned in the search for an answer to the continuing silence, had written a personal letter to the President of the United States, where the fate of the Franklin expedition was almost as keen a topic for discussion as on the eastern side of the Atlantic. She had requested that American whaling captains be officially informed of the offered rewards. One outcome of her request was that Henry Grinnell, president of the American Geographical and Statistical Society, detailed two small schooners to search for the crews if they could be found. The United States Navy Department provided the crews and also supplies for the Grinnell ships.

Another schooner engaged in the search was of only ninety tons. It was fitted out and sent to the Arctic at Lady Franklin's personal expense.

But by 1850 hope of finding the expedition or even survivors of it was beginning to flicker like a lamp running short of oil. Five years had passed without any word being received in England about the fate of Franklin and his men. The first news that the searchers had discovered evidence of the lost expedition was when Captain Horatio Austin, in command of four ships, two sailing vessels, H.M.S. *Assistance* and *Resolute*, and two small steamers, H.M.S. *Pioneer* and *Intrepid*, reported that he had found where Franklin and his ships had wintered in 1845–46, at Beechey Island, which was at the southern opening of Wellington Channel. The evidence was convincing. It included three graves of men who had succumbed to the Arctic weather and a considerable number of empty meat tins which had been filled with gravel.

Immediately the news reached England there was an outcry, for it was pointed out that the tins had contained more meat than the expedition could have been expected to consume that first winter, and much of it was of a brand that had been supplied to the Royal Navy and later found to be rotten when the tins were opened.

Had the expedition been supplied with rotten meat that had been condemned, forcing the men at Beechey Island to use up stores intended for later use?

If this had indeed been the case, then from the first days of that winter starvation might have become a spectre staring at men whose only hope was to hunt for food. Captain Austin searched Beechey Island for some concealed record but failed to find any. What had happened still remained a mystery. He wintered with his ships in Barrow Strait and when spring came dispatched many search parties, some by sea, others across the land mass. All these searches returned to base with nothing to report. They had not sighted so much as a cairn (a heap of stones), the usual method of marking a grave or a place where a record of passing has been left.

Having done all he could, Austin brought his ships home.

More English and American searchers set out in 1851. Some made fresh discoveries to alter the shape of maps of the Arctic, but none returned with news of the lost expedition. The *Prince Albert*, after taking an expedition raised by public contributions, returned again to the Arctic, this time in the command of a Canadian who was part Indian. This was Captain William Kennedy, whose second in command was a young French naval officer, Joseph-René Bellot. Kennedy decided to winter in Prince Regent Inlet, and in the next spring of 1852 went exploring on foot. This expedition returned after having discovered a new stretch of water that was named Bellot Strait.

Meanwhile in England Lieutenant Bedford Clapperton Pim had had an original idea. The Franklin expedition might have reached the coast of Siberia. With the backing of the Royal Geographical Society and funds provided by Lady Franklin and the Prime Minister, Pim journeyed to St. Petersburg full of hope. Not long afterwards he was back in London, having failed to secure permission to enter Siberia from the Czarist administration. He returned to Lady Franklin the money she had given him for his proposed venture.

Even on humanitarian grounds the Russians were not prepared to allow foreigners access to Siberia. More than a century and a revolutionary regime later that attitude of national isolation has not changed.

In 1853 the Hudson's Bay Company dispatched Dr. John Rae to the western coat of Boothia, for gradually all the known Arctic was being covered by the searchers wishing to unravel the mystery of what happened to the lost expedition, Rae's new expedition had some remarkable results. First, it made the discovery that King William Land, which had up till then been drawn on maps as part of Boothia, was actually an island. Then, after wintering in the North, in April 1854, in Pelly Bay, on the King William Land coast, Rae came upon some Eskimos who told him a story that could have been the first real news of the lost expedition.

According to the Eskimos Rae had met, another party of Eskimo seal hunters had four years before come upon a large party of about forty white men on the northern shore of King William Land. The white men were dragging a boat across the snow. None of them could speak more than a few words of the Eskimo language, but they had managed to convey to the surprised seal hunters that the ships they had journeyed in had been crushed in the Arctic pack ice. The impression they gave the Eskimo hunters was that they were making for a place where they believed there were deer.

When the Eskimo hunters returned to their village they said the white men had been thin and gaunt-looking. They had very few provisions and had been glad to buy a seal from the hunters.

Rae lost no time in trying to check this story and in trying to find out what happened to the party of white men with the boat.

He found other Eskimos who told him that later in that same year of 1850 another party of Eskimo hunters had come upon the bodies of thirty white men on the mainland and of another five on a small island off the coast. When Rae inquired precisely where, the best information he could gain was that the bodies were about a long day's journey from the Great Fish River.

The white men were dragging a boat across the snow.

What was most disturbing was the insistence of the Eskimos telling him of the finding of those bodies that all the white men had died of starvation, but not before some had begun cutting up several of the bodies for food.

Rae did his best to find other Eskimos with their own story of the finding of the bodies, but the only Eskimos he spoke to had the story at second hand from the first party who had made the discovery. So there was no real confirmation from an independent source of the claim that the last survivors had been reduced to cannibalism. Indeed, Rae was unable to locate any Eskimos who had been with the hunters who had come across the bodies, but he found that the story had regular currency among those he met. Indeed, the white men who had died as victims of the Far North had become a local legend among the Eskimos of King William Land, for many of their possessions had been found by the Eskimo hunters and four years later were being exchanged among the Eskimos Rae had met. He was shown broken and rusty watches, pieces of telescopes and guns, needles and cases of dismantled compasses, as well as spoons and forks of silver, some with crests of their former owners' families.

Rae bought a number of these articles of silverware and a round silver plate.

There was no point in remaining longer. Rae had found what he had come to find, evidence of the disaster that had overtaken the survivors of the ill-starred expedition that sailed with such high hopes to find the north-west Passage.

He was back in London in October of that same year of 1854. After leaving his ship he hastened to the Admiralty, where he delivered his prepared report on the outcome of his expedition. After being read and approved it was sent to *The Times* for publication.

When he saw it the editor was almost reduced to biting his fingernails. Only the previous day the paper had loosed one of its journalistic bolts on the subject of the lost expedition and had stated firmly that it was 'wellnigh as reasonable to look for the discovery of La Perouse as for any traces of poor Franklin and his followers'. The reference was to a loss that had continued for seventy years.

The following day an editor 'ate his own words'.

However, the excitement and sense of loss felt by the entire nation was mixed with feelings of horror and resentment. Rae had not spared any thought for the feelings of the lost crews' relatives, or if he had he had discounted them. He had included in his report the Eskimo story that the last survivors had resorted to cannibalism. Journals all over the country took him to task. Foremost in the attack on Rae for a seeming lack of sensitivity was Charles Dickens' *Household Words*, which in its issue of December 2, 1854, decided, on the strength of the report just published, there was 'no reason whatever to believe that any members of the expedition prolonged their existence by the dreadful expedient of eating the bodies of their dead companions'.

Dickens attacked the Eskimo story passed on by word of mouth as unreliable and pointed out that any observed wounds might have been caused by such animals as bears or wolves or foxes, possibly even by scurvy or the Eskimos themselves.

'It is the highest degree improbable,' the famous novelist insisted, 'that such men as the officers and crews of the two lost ships would, or could, in any extremity of hunger, alleviate the pains of starvation by this horrible means.'

Rae didn't receive this kind of attack without issuing a counter-blast. After asserting that he had been at great pains to check whatever he could through an excellent interpreter, he posed a question of his own.

'What possible motive,' he asked, 'could the Eskimo have for inventing such an awful tale?' Then went on to declaim, 'Alas, these poor people know too well what starvation is in its utmost extreme to be mistaken on such a point.'

He was suggesting indirectly that the Eskimo were cannibals, which was widening rather much the issue to which he had given rise.

The mystery of just how that vanished expedition came to face such disaster has never been adequately explained, nor has the mystery of whether some members of the crew became cannibals before they gave in to the fate of all. Certainly Franklin's biographers ignored that part of Rae's report that had been criticized by Charles Dickens and many others.

Of one fact there can be no dispute. The silverware established the names of some members of the expedition, for the crests and initials on the forks and spoons brought back by Rae were identified by members of the dead men's families. As for the silver plate Rae had been at pains to secure, it had Franklin's own name on it and among the fifty items he had bought from the Eskimos was Franklin's star of the Order of Hanover.

When he reached London Rae did not know that during his absence the reward offered by the Admiralty for positive information about the fate of the lost expedition had been increased to £10,000. He put in a formal claim for this sum and in due course received £8000. The remaining £2000 was distributed among the men who had made up his crew.

In the following year, 1855, the Admiralty sent another expedition under a Hudson's Bay man, James Anderson, to begin a fresh exploration, starting at the Great Fish River. The specific object of the Anderson party was to try to find lost records or documents left by the last survivors of Franklin's men. Anderson had no luck and returned without achieving anything of note to further the small store of knowledge about what happened to the most painfully remembered of all Arctic expeditions. If Sir John Franklin kept a diary it was not found, like that other famous diary kept by a famous Antarctic explorer, Captain Robert Falcon Scott, who with members of his party fell victim to a polar blizzard more than sixty years later.

In England Lady Franklin insisted on believing that her husband still might have survived in some miraculous fashion. Or if he had indeed perished, then she wanted him credited with having discovered that legendary north-west Passage. This discovery had been formally accorded by the Admiralty to Captain Robert McClure in H.M.S. *Investigator*, one of the naval vessels sent on a relief expedition. Just before Horatio Austin had set out McClure had gone to Bering Strait towards the end of 1850. He had done so against orders. Continuing, he had turned north-east and entered Prince of Wales Strait, between Banks and Victoria Islands, where winter had closed down on him. Early in the spring of 1851 he got his ship away from the ice and started down the west side of Banks Island, where he had to turn east looking for refuge in bad weather and found it in a harbour he discovered and named appropriately the Bay of God's Mercy.

Later the man who had disobeyed orders was credited with first sailing through the North-west Passage after discovering two routes from the North American mainland to Melville Island, which is north-east of that stretch of water north of Banks Island called McClure Strait, beyond which, sailing westward, lies the Beaufort Sea and the route to Alaska—in short, the north-west Passage.

However, Lady Franklin's determination to render to her husband the credit she felt due to him had an astonishing sequel. She wrote an impassioned letter to Lord Palmerston to send yet another expedition to the Arctic to seek further news of the lost expedition 'to satisfy,' she claimed, 'the honour of our country and clear up a mystery which has excited the sympathy of the civilized world.'

When this appeal brought no helpful response she decided to organize yet another public effort, financed by herself and various private contributions. With the money raised in this way she purchased a steam yacht of one hundred and seventy-seven tons and had it provisioned for a full two-year voyage. Captain Leopold McLintock, who had already been engaged on exploration in the Arctic, was offered the command of this vessel, the *Fox*, and accepted it.

Lady Franklin gave him his final instructions. They were to rescue any survivors of the lost expedition, recover any remaining records, and then to establish if possible if her husband had discovered the North-west Passage.

The *Fox* left Aberdeen on the 1st July, 1857, and eventually, after being trapped in the ice for two hundred and fifty-two days of the following autumn and winter, reached Beechey Island, where Franklin had spent the winter of 1845–46, more than eleven years before. Almost the first task McClintock undertook was the erection of a marble tablet given him by Lady Franklin. It bore an inscription to the memory of her husband and his companions.

When the winter of 1858 closed in McClintock organized a number of sledging forays, and on one of these across Prince of Wales Island he fell in with another group of Eskimos who had with them more of the lost expedition's personal effects. McClintock undertook to barter for more spoons and forks, which were readily exchanged for needles. A more memorable article he obtained was a silver medal that had belonged to the assistant surgeon of the *Terror*. It was from these Eskimos that he learned the story of a three-masted ship that had been crushed by the ice on the west coast of King William Island and sank, but all the white men aboard her had landed safely. From another party of Eskimos he learned that a second ship had been driven ashore on King William Island and had broken up. In the wreck of that ship had been found the body of a tall white man with very long teeth.

This seemed confirmation enough of what had happened and McClintock arranged for himself and Lieutenant William Hobson, his second in command, to take two separate parties to King William Island in an attempt to find some remains of the ship that had broken up. Stores of food and supplies were hidden, to be used later, and then the parties set out, McClintock along the eastern shore, Hobson along the western.

McClintock came upon an Eskimo village with about forty inhabitants, from whom he learned that the wrecked ships had been on the other side of the island, about five days' journey. He found little because the Eskimos had collected anything they considered of value before the wrecks vanished. However, he came upon a human skeleton lying face down in the ice. It appeared to be the remains of a European.

It was Lieutenant Hobson who finally discovered evidence of Franklin's death, though not a record of what happened to the lost expedition. Near Point Victory, on the north-west coast, he found a cairn which had been built by an earlier explorer, Sir James Ross. In the cairn had been thrust a bottle which contained two messages, both on the kind of printed form that was customarily placed in bottles and thrown overboard to help researchers determine tidal drifts and the course of currents.

The first message was headed with the date—May 28th, 1847, and briefly related that *Erebus* and *Terror* had been icebound at Beechey Island for their first winter after having cruised through Wellington Channel and returned down the west coast of Cornwallis Island. The second winter had been spent in latitude seventy degrees five minutes North and longitude ninety-eight degrees twenty-three minutes West. This message ended with the words:

'Sir John Franklin commanding the Expedition. All's Well.' It was signed by Lieutenant Graham Gore and Charles F. des Voeux, a mate.

The second message was written as a fill-in along the margin of the first. It was dated April 25, 1848, eleven months later, and was signed by the captains of the *Erebus* and *Terror*, Fitzjames and Crozier. It recorded simply:

'H.M. ships *Terror* and *Erebus* were deserted on the 22nd of April, five leagues N.N.W. of this, having been beset since 12th September, 1846 . . . The officers and crews, consisting of 105 souls, under the command of Captain F. R. M. Crozier, landed here. . . . Sir John Franklin died on the 11th June 1847, and the total loss by deaths in the expedition has been to this date 9 officers and 15 men. Start on tomorrow, 26th, for Back's Fish River.'

When he read these messages, brought to him by Hobson, McClintock decided that Sir John Franklin should be credited with having found the north-west Passage. He and Hobson both searched a wide area thoroughly in the hope of coming across another cairn and records of the expedition, but they were disappointed.

The cairn concealing the bottle was a bare fifteen miles from where the ships sank and were abandoned, but the evidence of discarded cooking stoves, tools, nautical instruments, a pile of clothing four feet high, even a medicine case, told its own story. The expedition members had been over-burdened and unable to make real progress on foot.

The morning after the discovery of the cairn McClintock came upon the shell of the boat the survivors had been seen hauling with them by the seal hunters. It was mounted on a heavy sledge and was pointing north. Inside were two skeletons, a few books, and five watches, as well as two double-barrelled guns and a modest supply of tea and chocolate. One barrel of each of the guns had been discharged.

The other was loaded and, rather curiously, at full cock, ready for firing.

When McClintock arrived back in England with his story and relics he had a tale to tell which showed to those who pieced together the jigsaw of the expedition's progress that Franklin could have died within a hundred miles of his goal, beaten by the ice which proved too much for his low-powered auxiliary engines. The last survivors were actually within sight of the American mainland. They were men who were being forced to endure a third winter in the Arctic. They had not the strength, only the will, and that was not enough, as Captain Scott's ill-fated party demonstrated in 1912.

But why did their food supplies give out? Therein lies the very core of the Franklin mystery. Was it because they found on Beechey Island that their tins of meat were all rotten and had to be discarded? If so, who was responsible for provisioning the two lost ships with food not fit for human consumption and so risking the lives of more than a hundred gallant men?

Why did Franklin himself leave no record? Was he too overcome by a prospect filled with despair? No graves were marked on land and no cairns were set up. Again why?

It was a well-organized and certainly well-disciplined expedition, yet disaster seems to have overcome it almost too easily. There was no record left on Beechey Island and there still is no answer to a mystery that has puzzled generations since the middle of the nineteenth century. Why were the ships abandoned so early in the year?

Had the crushing ice of previous months locked in the pack made them unseaworthy?

Was that the reason they made such slow progress in the summer of 1846, when Peel strait was navigated, so that from the spring until mid-September only two hundred miles were traversed?

The real mystery of this truly grim and sad story is that there are no answers to these questions. Like the north-west Passage it set out hopefully to find and navigate, the expedition that vanished has with the passage of time acquired the quality of legend.

STAY ON TARGET

Here are details of other exciting TARGET titles. If you cannot obtain these books from your local bookshop, or newsagent, write to the address below listing the titles you would like and enclosing cheque or postal order—*not* currency—including 7p per book to cover packing and postage; 2–4 books, 5p per copy; 5–8 books, 4p per copy.

TARGET BOOKS,
Universal-Tandem Publishing Co.,
14 Gloucester Road,
London SW7 4RD

HAUNTED HOUSES 30p
Bernhardt J. Hurwood
0 426 10559 1 **A Target Mystery**
Who was the ghost of Powis Castle? Why has he not been seen for 200 years? What was the cause of the fatal curse on Mouse Tower? And why does Anne Boleyn ride headless with a coach and four around the grounds of Blicking Hall? Here are 25 spine-chilling tales to spirit you away . . . into HAUNTED HOUSES! *Illustrated.*

THE LONDON QUIZ BOOK 30p

R. W. Wilson

0 426 10436 6

Going on a day visit or holiday to London? Have fun by asking your friends, and yourself for that matter, questions about this most exciting of all the capital cities in the world! Questions on: Royal London; Government; Law and Order; museums; the Thames; zoos and parks; statues; famous buildings; ancient traditions and so forth . . . *Illustrated.*

DOCTOR WHO AND THE SEA-DEVILS 30p

Malcolm Hulke

0 426 10516 8 **A Target Adventure**

Whilst visiting the MASTER, who has been exiled to a luxurious castle prison on a small island, DOCTOR WHO and Jo Grant learn that a number of ships have vanished in the area. Whilst investigating these mysterious disappearances Jo and the Doctor are attacked by a SEA DEVIL, one of many who plan to conquer the earth, aided and abetted by the evil MASTER! *Illustrated.*

DOCTOR WHO AND THE DÆMONS 30p

Barry Letts

0 426 10444 7 **A Target Adventure**

DOCTOR WHO is strangely concerned about Professor Horner's plan to cut open an ancient barrow near Devil's End; equally worried is Miss Hawthorne, the local white witch, who foretells a terrible disaster if he goes ahead; determined that he should is Mr. Magister, the new vicar (in truth the MASTER) whose secret ceremonies are designed to conjure up from out of the barrow a horribly powerful being from a far-off planet. An exciting adventure with the forces of black magic! *Illustrated.*

COMMANDOS IN ACTION! 35p

Graeme Cook

0 426 10508 7 **Target True-life Adventure**

True stories of Britain's immortal Commando Regiment—the crack military unit whose skill, determination and courage did so much to hamper Hitler's efforts to conquer this country during the Second World War. *Illustrated.*

SEA-GREEN MAGIC 30p

Elisabeth Beresford

0 426 10479 x **A Target Adventure**

In which Johnny finds a funny, square-shaped bottle with a strange misty look about it whilst exploring sea-side rock pools. Imprisoned inside is an Arabian Djinn, or genie, who when released is destined to create some awkward problems for Johnny, Lorna and Alan. *Illustrated.*

SKIPPER TO THE RESCUE! 30p

Judith M. Berrisford

0 426 10495 1 **Target Animal Fiction**

Bad news! The Appleby farmstead is in danger of having to be sold off, so it's Skipper, Roddy, Jane, Kitty and Pete—to the rescue! Whilst the children are busy trying to raise money to help the farm out of its difficulties, Skipper does a little extra rescue work of his own and ends up winning the Blue Cross Medal! . . . *The second adventure in this famous series. Illustrated.*

SKIPPER—THE DOG FROM THE SEA 30p

Judith M. Berrisford

0 426 10487 0 **Target Animal Fiction**

A strange white Alsatian dog visits the Appleby seaside farmstead by moonlight. Whose dog is he? Will he make friends with the four Appleby children—Roddy, Jane, Kitty and Pete? What is the mystery behind him? The Appleby family have some exciting moments in this thrilling story before they find the answers to these questions. . . . *The first adventure in this famous series. Illustrated.*

ABANDONED! 25p

G. D. Griffiths

0 426 10460 9

A kitten, heartlessly abandoned when 12 weeks old, gradually accepts the loss of her comfort and security, and learns to survive in the grim and savage wilds of storm-racked Dartmoor, several times cheating a cruel death before eventually finding the love and security she secretly longs for. *Illustrated.*

RUNNER-UP TITLE FOR THE 1973 WHITBREAD LITERARY AWARD (CHILDREN'S BOOK DIVISION)

WELL MET BY WITCHLIGHT 30p

Nina Beachcroft

0 426 10356 4 **A Target Adventure**

In which Sarah, Christopher and Lucy meet a strange little old woman called Mary, a 'white' witch who can tame animals, raise wind and water, change her shape and, yes—actually fly on a broomstick! Whether or not she can deal with the evil-eyed Mrs Bella Black, a very powerful 'black' witch who lives in the next village, is another matter which concerns the children very much as they are caught up into the middle of a terrifyingly dangerous battle fought out between the two witches on the supernatural plane.

THAT MAD, BAD BADGER 25p

Molly Burkett

0 426 10399 4

A blow-by-blow true account of life with 'Nikki' the badger, who delights in whipping laces out of the shoes of unsuspecting visitors to the Burkett household, stealing goodies from the 'fridge, and lying tummyside-up in a comfortable armchair for a quiet snooze. There have been other stories about badgers, but never one like this! *Illustrated.*

ROCKET TO FAME 25p

John Rowland

0 426 10401 3

Here is the dramatic story of the man who was architect of Britain's world-famous railway system—George Stephenson, whose famous 'Rocket' won the great locomotive competition of 1829—the story of a genius who grasped hold of his destiny with both hands and within the space of a few years transformed the life of a nation! *Illustrated.*

GHOSTS, GHOULS, AND OTHER HORRORS 25p

Bernhardt J. Hurwood

0 426 10321 1 **A Target Mystery**

50 true, scarifying stories of the supernatural collected from Britain, Europe, America and other parts of the world. Shudder happily with these eerie tales of phantoms, headless apparitions, vampires and werewolves, and don't forget to turn the light out! *Illustrated.*